"I loved reading *Moving from ALERT to Acceptance: Helping Clinicians Heal from Client Suicide*. Khara Croswaite Brindle's book is a map for psychotherapists and other mental health workers to follow when working with this population. Croswaite Brindle did a beautiful job describing therapists' and clients' pain, internal dialogue, and what-ifs. This book provides helpful and straightforward tips for therapists to know and follow, including definitions, questions, and acronyms."

—Liliana Baylon, LMFT-S, RPT-S, bilingual and bicultural psychotherapist and consultant

MOVING FROM ALERT TO ACCEPTANCE

Helping Clinicians Heal from Client Suicide

KHARA CROSWAITE BRINDLE

ROWMAN & LITTLEFIELD
Lanham • Boulder • New York • London

Published by Rowman & Littlefield
An imprint of The Rowman & Littlefield Publishing Group, Inc.
4501 Forbes Boulevard, Suite 200, Lanham, Maryland 20706
www.rowman.com

86-90 Paul Street, London EC2A 4NE

British Library Cataloguing in Publication Information available

Library of Congress Cataloging-in-Publication Data

Names: Brindle, Khara Croswaite, author.
   Title: Moving from ALERT to acceptance : helping clinicians heal from client
   suicide / Khara Croswaite Brindle.
Description: Lanham : Rowman & Littlefield, [2024] | Includes bibliographical
   references and index.
Identifiers: LCCN 2023058553 (print) | LCCN 2023058554 (ebook) |
   ISBN 9781538188620 (cloth) | ISBN 9781538188637 (paperback) | ISBN
   9781538188644 (epub)
Subjects: LCSH: Suicide—Prevention. | Suicidal behavior—Diagnosis. | Suicidal
   behavior—Treatment. | Psychotherapist and patient. | Psychotherapists—Job
   stress. | Suicide victims.
Classification: LCC RC569 .B745 2024 (print) | LCC RC569 (ebook) | DDC
   362.28—dc23/eng/20240301
LC record available at https://lccn.loc.gov/2023058553
LC ebook record available at https://lccn.loc.gov/2023058554

Contents

Introduction
I'm Part of the Statistic

I'M PART OF THE STATISTIC, the one that says 25% of clinicians will lose a client to suicide in their career (McAdams & Foster 2000). This book isn't about academia or research on suicide; it's about hurt, heart, and healing. Because although there are many books out there that discuss suicide risks and assessment needs (see Appendixes A and B), there are limited resources that address the experience of a clinician losing a client to suicide and ways to heal from it. Fear and concerns of responsibility are keeping clinicians from sharing their experiences of suicide with others within their professional community. It's an experience Dr. Lena Salpietro and colleagues (2023) call confidential grief. As Kayla Weiner states in her book, *Therapeutic and Legal Issues for Therapists Who Have Survived a Client Suicide* (2005), "this topic has to be discussed openly so that therapists can get the support they need at this very difficult time." I wholeheartedly agree and plan to do just that. The aim of this book is to openly discuss the loss of a client to suicide from a compassionate and nonjudgmental lens for the providers who are grieving this loss alongside their client's family and/ or community. To sit alongside therapists like Jeremy, Lorel, Evie, Alejandra, and Annabelle. This book will approach this career-altering topic by (1) illustrating suicide risks through case studies of client suicidal thought, both chronic and acute, (2) exploring how communities and mental health leaders can help clinicians process this tragedy, and (3) offering healing strategies for clinicians who experience a client death by suicide.

Personal Reflection

I have to agree with Weiner (2005) when she says, "it seems impossible for a therapist to speak or write about her or his experience of surviving a client suicide without describing the event itself, as well as her or his healing in the process of regaining a sense of professional competence." This book has become a significant part of my own personal and professional healing journey from suicide loss. It's an invitation to join me on the emotional path of getting to know Rena, Tillie, and Marlena as beautiful, messy, hurting humans. This book is both an opportunity for healing and an exercise in tender vulnerability to be able to share my experience with client suicide so fully with you. I also recognize that by the time you finish reading this book, you will have your own thoughts and feelings about me as a therapist. I expect it. I encourage you to approach the content of this book from the three C's: compassion, curiosity, and critical thinking. By putting yourself in my shoes as the therapist of Rena, Tillie, and Marlena, you're accepting my gift of understanding, and I'm receiving yours.

Looking at Language

It's been known for years now how stigmatizing and hurtful the use of the phrase *committed suicide* can be. Therefore you will see the use of language like *client death by suicide* and *client suicide* to describe the experience of a client loss throughout this book. Being a suicide loss survivor both personally and professionally, I will also use language like *therapist survivor* to distinguish a therapist who has experienced a client loss to suicide rather than a personal loss. People can have both personal and professional losses and different responses to those losses. Additionally, although the term *suicidal ideation* is prevalent in professional texts and clinical circles, I prefer to use the term *suicidal thought* for two reasons. First, it conveys a gentleness to suicide questions that feels more personable and approachable in language choice when used by professionals asking about suicide. Second, the use of the word *ideation* can lead to confusion for clients who've never heard the term used before, and worst-case scenario, using the term *ideation* leads to a disconnection between clients and providers when there's fear of stigma surrounding suicide. Should you rise to the challenge of trying out *suicidal thought* in your verbal interactions with clients when asking about suicide, or should you choose to experiment with it in writing within your intake forms, I invite you to notice the meaningful shift away from stigma toward comfort for both yourself and your client.

The Challenges of Suicide Prevention

As we move through this book, I will be touching on aspects of what we know about suicide in this moment, with new findings from research coming out regularly that adds to our awareness and understanding of suicide and suicide prevention. We know that suicide doesn't discriminate in that it has touched individuals and communities of all backgrounds, beliefs, genders, ages, races, and ethnicities. We also know that young people are more likely to be impulsive from a developmental lens, which adds to the tragedy that is youth suicide. We know that impulsivity can prevent suicide response and support from others including therapists, and this inability to help because folks aren't telling us they are suicidal scares us. There is a small population that has an idea of suicide and attempts suicide within minutes. These folks are outliers in the suicide prevention conversation, eliminating our ability to help because they've made a decision to die and aren't telling anyone. There is a bigger population of people who we can help because they've experienced suicidal thoughts for weeks, months, or years and are willing to talk to us about it. These are the folks we will focus on throughout this book.

Book Layout

This book can feel like two books in one. In Part I: *Head*, we walk through the steps of a suicide assessment and explore key risk factors for suicide. We get to know Rena, Tillie, and Marlena as clients experiencing suicidal thoughts. Under the surface, the title speaks to how we choose to operate as professionals, meaning we like logic and operating from intelligence found within our professional minds. We seek to demystify suicide by comprehending facts and figures. We want thought to dictate our actions, not emotions. When it comes to suicide, we may crave protocols to feel safe in something that still feels unpredictable and scary. If you are seeking answers to the experience that is suicide within the mental health profession, I invite you to start with Part I. If you feel that you are well versed in suicide and suicide assessment, you may choose to skip ahead to Part II: *Heart*. If you are currently going through the grief process of losing a client to suicide, Part II is for you. *Heart* holds the symptoms of grief and loss a professional can experience after a client suicide. It speaks to the disruption and heaviness of heart a clinician can experience. It explores how communities and mental health leaders can help a clinician grow in the aftermath of this tragedy. Part II introduces us to fellow therapists Annabelle, Evie, Alejandra, Jeremy, and Lorel, who have experienced a client suicide. *Heart* also introduces grief and loss tools a clinician can embrace as part of their personal healing journey. *Heart* speaks to the heart energy of suicide and suicide loss. It captures the emotions and the pain, and the humanness of the experience where logic doesn't necessarily reign. As humans, we need both head and heart to exist together. As professionals, we need both head and heart to work with clients effectively. As therapist survivors, we need both head and heart to heal.

Identity Protection

Although this book features clinician and client experiences with suicide, I have omitted or changed identifying details including names to protect their identities. Any resemblance to actual persons, places, or events is purely coincidental. Many additional details have been altered to protect identity, and some of the people described in this book are composites based on several different people I've worked with professionally.

Part I

HEAD

Meet Rena, Tillie, and Marlena 1

Rena

RENA SAT ACROSS from me decked out in her favorite color, green. This color made her eyes appear golden, like the eyes of a lion. She stated that she'd had to find a new therapist because her therapist of several years had moved away. She was forthcoming in sharing her trauma history, including an extensive family history of physical and emotional abuse, as well as several sexual assaults in childhood and young adulthood. Her verbal delivery of each traumatic event felt a bit jarring at first, mainly because she stated each painful thing from an aloof, distant place, as if it had happened to someone else. I vividly recall how her lion eyes stared back at me with cool regard, measuring my reaction to each trauma she shared. When asked about her goals for therapy, Rena stated that she wanted to heal from the estrangement she'd enforced with her abusers. She wanted to work through her traumas. She wanted to have a baby with her spouse. "Otherwise," she stated so matter-of-factly, "my suicidal thoughts will win."

Tillie

Tillie had come to therapy at the request of both her parents. As a 12-year-old girl, she first presented as nervous and soft-spoken, with a smattering of freckles across her nose. As we built more therapeutic rapport, she revealed more of her true personality, which included a wonderful sense of humor, a love of cats and softball, being with her friends, and making art. Then one session she came in looking like a different person. Her hair was cut short and hung haphazardly around her shoulders. She avoided eye contact. She sat down on the couch, folded into herself, and began to cry. "My parents are getting a divorce," she said between sobs. "It's all my fault. They'd be better off without me."

Marlena

Marlena came into therapy wearing bright, bold jewelry and stated she wanted to work on a recent breakup. As a middle-aged woman, Marlena shared that her greatest accomplishments were earning a graduate degree in women's studies and having her daughter at home. Although Marlena stated she had a goal to start her own business, she disclosed a history of unhealthy relationships flavored with codependency and abuse patterns that kept her from positions of power and made her question if things were worth the effort. When asked about her supports, Marlena shared that she only had her daughter by her side. "I've been suicidal for eight years," she said. "I have to wait until my daughter is 18 before I can end it all."

Where do we begin as professionals in response to client disclosures of suicidal thought? What bells go off in your head as the mental health professional serving these clients? If you were lucky, you received a robust training in suicide assessment and safety planning in graduate school. You feel prepared. You're ready to go there. However, more often than not, I hear that clinicians received an hour-long lecture in graduate school that resulted in solidifying messages of fear, "cover your ass," and "hospitalize." That's not enough time in suicide training and that's not the right message for therapists to receive. I personally believe Dr. Stacey Freedenthal says it best in her book, *Helping the Suicidal Person* (2018), when she emphasizes the importance of showing up for clients by leaning into a client's suicide story. How did they get here? What's going on that is making suicide a possibility? Yes, we need to ask some questions and listen for risk factors. Yes, we need to ask about thoughts, means, and intent. And yet there's so much more to consider than just a cold clinical checklist when exploring client risks for suicide.

Engaging a Suicidal Person 2

WHAT DO WE DO when Rena reports "suicidal thoughts will win," or when Tillie states that her parents will be better off without her? What's your next question for Marlena when she states she's staying alive until her daughter becomes an adult? How comfortable are you asking about suicide? What are ways you can lean in? Consider the following on your journey to becoming more comfortable with speaking of suicide with clients.

Clinician Confidence

How confident are you in asking about suicide? Do you stumble over your words? Hesitate? Struggle with eye contact? Do you ask about self-harm but don't explicitly ask about suicide? Do you ask about clients hurting themselves and think their "no" to self-harm is a definite "no" to suicide as well?

Trainer Tip: Suicide is one of several reasons people engage in self-harm. Self-harm does not always mean suicide.

Mannerisms and Body Language

What does your body do when you ask about suicide? Do you find your shoulders going up to your ears? Are you fidgeting? Wiggling your leg? Clenching your hands? Is your body language closed? Do you look scared or uncomfortable to your client?

Trainer Tip: Adrenaline can reduce our control over our bodies. Try to ground yourself with your feet on the floor, leaning in slightly toward your client to convey you are present and in this conversation with them.

Direct Questions

How do you ask about suicide? Do you ask directly or do you have the urge to circle around it? Do you feel that you need to soft pitch the idea of suicide such as asking if they want to hurt themselves? Can you normalize suicidal thought in how you ask it? What words can you use? Why did you pick those words?

Examples of direct questions about suicide:

1. Are you thinking of suicide?
2. Are you having thoughts of suicide?
3. Are you thinking of dying?
4. Is suicide a part of your experience?
5. Others who've experienced something like this have had thoughts of suicide. What about you? (soft pitch example)

Trainer Tip: Asking a client if they want to hurt themselves doesn't actually lend clarity to suicidal thought or suicide risks. A concrete thinker can truthfully say "no" to wanting to hurt themselves and answer "yes" to wanting to die. Direct questions matter!

Environment or Safety of Space

In what environment is the conversation around suicide taking place? Is there privacy? Confidentiality? Do you have an office with a door that can be closed? Are you in a school where your client might worry they'll be overheard by staff or peers? What do you have in your office that conveys safety and trust when talking about suicide?

Trainer Tip: Clients notice what books you have on your shelves. Do you have titles they can see about suicide? Have you normalized that conversations about suicide are welcome in therapy as part of your intake in wanting to be of help? Efforts like these can give a client increased comfort in knowing you are willing to talk about suicide.

Rena

"Thank you for your honesty about having suicidal thoughts, Rena. Can you tell me more about them?" My response and invitation to Rena came from a place of compassion and curiosity, which she could see in my open body language and eye contact. She felt invited to elaborate, which, as her new therapist, helped me learn that her suicidal thoughts were chronic and had been with her since she was 13 years old. She named how they got louder when in a fight with her spouse or after getting an unwanted social media message from an estranged family member. Rena was also able to share that she'd made two suicide attempts since she was 13, one resulting in a hospital stay in her late teens.

Tillie

"I can see how distressed you are, Tillie. I'm so sorry this is happening. Can you help me understand what you mean when you say your parents would be better off without you?" Tillie looked up at me through her tears and seemed reassured by what she saw on my face. "I want to die," she said.

Marlena

"I get the sense that you know your suicidal thoughts very well in handling them these past eight years, Marlena. You've shared that your daughter is keeping you alive and that you are waiting to die until she's 18. Can you tell me how old she is now?" Every time I share Marlena's story in a suicide assessment training, my peers correctly focus on how old her daughter is in the moment. After all, she's Marlena's primary protective factor, and I need to ask questions to better understand the mother-daughter dynamics as well as the timeline I have to work with as Marlena's current therapist. By creating a space of safety, I'm inviting Marlena to disclose more in order to build rapport and appropriately assess her risks for suicide.

Both your comfort and your client's comfort talking about suicide come with time and trust. Practicing your questions about suicide may be a valuable piece to this puzzle. I recall how *LivingWorks* ASIST Training starts Day 1 of training with repeated role-play practice asking about suicide until it gets easier to ask. Finding ourselves repeating the question until it's said with confidence instead of shakiness. This practice stuck with me as such a simple and valuable strategy for professional helpers! It also helps to have a framework that makes all the important pieces of suicide assessment easy to remember, especially as the human side of us hears our heartbeat loudly in our ears when a client answers "yes" to current thoughts of suicide.

A Is for Ask 3

R ECOGNIZING HOW ALERT and anxious we can feel as mental health professionals asking about suicide, I made it my mission to help colleagues feel more comfortable with the process. One way this can happen more easily is by introducing them to my ALERT acronym for suicide assessment and safety planning.

A is for Ask
L is for Listen
E is for Engage
R is for Respond
T is for Tasks

As we've already begun to name, suicide is a human experience, and it is much more than a checklist on suicidal thought, means, plans, and intent. Here are some additional things to ask about in order to more fully understand a person's current experience with suicide.

Frequency/Controllability/Duration

How often are you having suicidal thoughts?
How easy or difficult are the thoughts to control?
How long do the thoughts last?

Trainer Tip: As you start to conceptualize risk, how different is it to hear a client say they had one thought of suicide a year ago that lasted a matter of seconds versus a client who shares suicide is constantly with them, with thoughts occurring daily for hours on end?

Visual/Imagery

When you think about suicide, what do you see (Freedenthal 2018)? What comes to mind when you think of dying by suicide? Visuals or imagery can tell us a lot about our client's experience. You might be surprised by what you hear when asking this modern question within suicide assessment.

Trainer Tip: Inviting clients to share imagery can add context to the conversation of suicide, including themes of relief, pain, or reuniting with loved ones.

Personal Meaning

What would suicide mean for you?
What pieces need clarification for me to understand what you are going through?
Similar to the visual question, what context can be added by their elaborated response? Is it about pain? Escaping? Ending? Reuniting?

Trainer Tip: Suicide is more about ending pain than it is about death (Freedenthal 2023). Do you clearly hear aspects of pain in their sharing? Why or why not?

Exposure to Suicide

Do you know someone who has died by suicide?
Is there suicide in your family?
Are you aware of suicides in your community?
How did people around you respond to learning of a death by suicide?

Trainer Tip: More exposure to suicide can add to risk in normalizing suicide as an option. Whether it's a cluster of suicides in mountain or rural communities, or multiple suicides within the family, asking about exposure is important.

Plan/Preparation

Do you have a plan to die? What steps have you taken with that plan?

Trainer Tip: Explore the lethality of the plan as they share it. Is there a difference for you as a professional hearing a client's plan to stop eating versus their plan to buy a gun to end their life?

Rehearsal

Have they rehearsed their suicide attempt in their mind?
Have they visited the location where they want to die?
Have they learned to tie a noose? Have they stockpiled pills? Have they loaded the gun?

Trainer Tip: People who are suffering with suicidal thoughts for weeks, months, or years tend to have a plan identified that may include visiting the location where they want to die. Is this true for your client? Why or why not?

Intent

Tell me about your intention to die.
What percentage of you wants to live and what percentage of you wants to die?
On a scale of 1 to 10, 1 being *not at all* and 10 being *any moment now*, what's your current intent to die?

Trainer Tip: Scaling suicidal urge and intent can simplify checking in on suicidal thoughts between sessions or week to week. This can be helpful when tracking clients with chronic suicidality to ensure nothing has changed that is adding more risk for suicide in the present moment.

Tillie

"Sounds like things have gotten pretty bad, Tillie, as I hear you saying you want to die. Can you tell me, in percentages, what amount of you wants to live and what amount of you wants to die?" When Tillie came into this session, her numbers were 40% wanting to live, 60% wanting to die. As we started talking about what was happening for her and the pain she was feeling, Tillie reported 50/50 with 5 out of

10 intent. As her therapist, I could have made the mistake of saying something like, "oh, you don't really want to die, you're just upset." Rather than discounting her experience, *I leaned in*, asking her to tell me more. Tillie reported a strong urge to self-harm in expression of the internal pain and anxiety she was feeling, having a history of self-harm that started at 11 years old that had stopped five months ago.

Rena

Engaging Rena more deeply in her suicide story uncovered low intent (2 out of 10), no plans and no means when starting therapy. In exploring triggers for her suicidal thoughts, Rena pinpointed that conflict with her spouse or unwanted contact from family brought on trauma flashbacks, hypervigilance, and self-criticism that sounded like her own voice saying, "You are so stupid, how could you let these things happen to you?" Rena felt helpless and overwhelmed by the voice inside her head that said she should have fought back rather than freeze in her trauma experiences as a child.

Marlena

"What does suicide mean for you?" It's the question I asked after learning that her daughter was 15 years old, confirming that we had some time to do this therapeutic work together. Marlena expressed chronic, recurring depression and feelings of fatigue when thinking about fighting for a life she wasn't even sure she wanted. We began to explore what had transpired within the last eight years for thoughts of suicide to be a regular but uninvited guest in Marlena's mind each day.

Asking for more information is always helpful to better understand a client's experience where suicide has become an option. It's also important to debunk the myth that asking about suicide gives someone the idea. Not true. If suicide isn't someone's experience, they will be quick to correct their clinician and move on. However, if suicide is in fact part of their experience, it can give them some relief to talk about it freely (Freedenthal 2023). Asking from a place of curiosity and compassion shows the client that you are in it with them, while also giving you much-needed context as the professional exploring the person's risk within your formal suicide assessment.

L Is for Listen

Now that we've modeled what it means to talk about suicide and ask about suicidal thought directly, there are several things to listen for when exploring a client's risk. It's important to name that there isn't one particular thing we are listening for when it comes to determining a client's risk for suicide. The more factors a client endorses, the more the metaphorical pile grows, leading to disruption, hopelessness, and pain with increased risks for suicide. Explore all the sources for risk factors of suicide in Appendix B. I invite you to listen closely for the following with your clients.

Suicidal Behaviors

Is this the first time your client has experienced suicidal thoughts? Do they have a history with suicide, whether it be thoughts, plans, or attempts? Have they experienced aborted or interrupted suicide attempts? Have they been hospitalized for suicidal thoughts or attempts?

Trainer Tip: A modern question in suicide assessment is to ask your client if they've googled anything related to suicide. If they say yes, what did they google? When looking at risk, it's going to land differently for you as their therapist if you hear they were googling the 9-8-8 hotline versus a client sharing they were googling to find a website that would teach them how to die by suicide.

Current/Past Mental Health Disorders

Would it surprise you to know that any mental health disorder increases risk for suicide? This comes from the lens of disorders or diagnoses indicating a significant level of disruption or dysfunction in a person's life. In other words, disruption or disfunction can add to the risk for suicide when we think of the impact on a person's quality of life and functioning. Mental health disorders increase risk, not as a cause-and-effect relationship with suicide, but as an item on the pile of risk factors we are identifying for each client.

With that being said, there are five mental health diagnoses (subject to change) that appear to have a more significant relationship to elevated suicide risk.

1. Major Depressive Disorder (MDD)
2. Post-Traumatic Stress Disorder (PTSD)
3. Substance Abuse
4. Bipolar Disorder
5. Borderline Personality Disorder (BPD)

What do all these diagnoses have in common? In addition to being disruptive to overall functioning, several of them can also have an aspect of sleep disruption. Of all the symptoms a client can report to their medical or mental health professional, sleep disruption is one to track closely because of the significant impact it has on physical and mental well-being. Sleep disruption can include insomnia, nightmares, night terrors, waking up frequently, poor sleep quality, absence of REM sleep, sleepwalking, and too little sleep. Sleep is foundational to functioning, and therefore contributes to mental health challenges and risks for suicide.

Trainer Tip: Ask about sleep regardless of whether there is a formal mental health diagnosis present or in your client's history. Sleep is an important factor when measuring progress with all therapeutic outcomes.

Symptoms

As mentioned above, sleep disruption is the number one symptom to be concerned about as it relates to suicide risk. Clients are likely to name symptoms to a helping professional, but aren't always forthcoming in the connection these symptoms have to suicidal thoughts. Why? People continue to fear that if they share their suicidal thoughts, the person they disclose this to will hospitalize them (Blanchard & Farber 2020). Additionally, prior to having intentional screeners for suicide as part of medical care, several studies showed that there were a handful of folks seeing their medical professional or going to the emergency room, only to die by suicide within 30 days of that visit due to not experiencing relief (Shea 2011, p. 7). Historically, professionals were not making the connection between client symptoms and their suicide. This is a tragic finding, and we have since been attempting to do better as professionals by having clients complete screeners and/or intentionally asking about suicide in these encounters.

Trainer Tip: Making the connection with clients between symptoms and suicide can feel a little disjointed at times. One idea is to have your client name all their symptoms, followed by reflecting on those symptoms and how other clients have had suicidal thoughts as part of those same symptoms. Are suicidal thoughts part of your client's experience? By asking it this way, your client is invited to share more, even if suicide is not a factor in what they are going through.

Family History

Many suicide loss survivors (people who have lost someone to suicide) may feel shocked to know that they are automatically categorized as higher risk for suicide if they've lost a close family member to suicide. Yet there are some interesting reasons behind this, including two possibilities of reuniting and modeling. When we invite a client to lean in further into their suicide story, they may report that they are missing their loved one so deeply, that they consider suicide as a way to reunite with them. Another client may say that, although it was beyond painful to lose their loved one to suicide, they can't help but see their loved one as someone who is no longer suffering, thus modeling that suicide is one way for the pain to end.

Trainer Tip: Although elevated risk is found with nuclear family members (Joiner 2005, p. 174), asking about any and all family members who have died by suicide can be an important conversation, especially if it invites the client to reflect on their own beliefs. It also serves to explore the messaging and responses of other surviving family members in response to each loss.

Access to Firearms

Firearms remain the most lethal means to die by suicide. We continue to see more adult males choose firearms over other means to die (American Association of Suicidology 2023). We also know that youth are accessing firearms in the afterschool hours when parental supervision is absent (Gorchynski & Anderson 2005). Therefore it's important to ask about access to firearms, not only in the primary residence, but at friend and family homes where the person may be spending time. Additionally, safety plans around firearms have evolved over the years. Now, instead of surrendering a firearm to law enforcement, professionals are working with clients to

(1) surrender the gun to a family member or trusted friend or (2) have the gun locked in a gun safe with ammunition stored separately. The American Association of Suicidology (2023) also reports that having ammunition stored separate from the gun buys more time when feeling a strong urge to kill oneself, with the barriers of time and effort to access all materials saving lives in comparison to immense pain, high impulsivity, and a loaded firearm found conveniently in the nightstand.

Trainer Tip: What safety plans can be in place for your client for securing firearms? Are they willing to lock the gun in a gun safe? Do they have a safety lock? Can ammunition be stored separately from the locked firearm? Do they have a trusted friend or family member who would hold onto it for them if things got worse?

Physical Illness

Physical illness includes several aspects to consider when evaluating risk for suicide. What usually comes to mind first is chronic pain. Since we know that suicide is more about escaping pain than it is about death, it's natural for suicidal thoughts to occur when someone is experiencing long-lasting, disruptive, excruciating pain that they feel isn't going to change. Additionally, physical illness can include terminal illness where an individual's quality of life is expected to decline. Per the Centers for Disease Control and Prevention (CDC 2023), we are seeing more older adults sixty-five and older choose to die by suicide, which could speak to a choice to end their lives rather than suffer through a significant decline in health.

Trainer Tip: Asking a client to scale their experience of physical pain can be helpful when exploring risk. A client who scales their pain as 7 out of 10 more days than not may have different thoughts on suicide than someone with pain that is 5 out of 10 that occurs 1–2x per month, as just one example.

Lack of Social Support

Dr. Jean Twenge is a researcher who has been tracking differences in various generations since the 1980s. Her research on the iGen/GenZ generation (Twenge 2017) indicates that they are reporting a lack of social connection and support. How does this elevate suicide risk? For some clients, it can reinforce internal beliefs that they wouldn't be missed or that no one would care if they were gone. In other words, a lack of social support may reinforce their internal beliefs of burdensomeness and insignificance to others. These beliefs can make it hard to identify viable supports in a safety plan. How can we best ask about supports for folks who feel they have none? Many people won't disclose suicide to someone due to fears of being hospitalized, but perhaps they can name that they are having a mental health day that requires distraction when engaging someone else. By sharing that, they are looking to get out of their own head. Can they invite someone to talk about themselves or anything else that can serve as a healthy distraction?

Trainer Tip: Instead of asking, "who are your supports?" consider asking, "who can provide a healthy distraction?" This reframing of the question of supports allows even the most isolated of clients to potentially identify a connection in their social world that might serve the purpose of healthy distraction, including a peer at school, a social media contact, or a video gaming colleague, to name a few.

Psychiatric Hospitalization

As we named in the suicidal behaviors section earlier in this chapter, a prior hospitalization for suicide increases suicide risk. Additionally, any hospitalization for mental health can also be an added risk factor for suicide, and there are several reasons why. First, the experience of a hospitalization can be stressful or traumatic. A client being hospitalized against their will, or feeling that their power or autonomy has been stripped from them, is understandably traumatic. Second, if they experienced a traumatic event while in the hospital, such as a physical or sexual assault, this could also contribute to increased suicide risk. Third, the stressors that contributed to a client's mental health crisis prior to hospitalization may still be present in their lives upon discharge, which wouldn't remove all suicide risks when they are sent home. Lastly, a medication change during their hospital stay could contribute to their suicidal thoughts if it causes additional disruption through side effects. More worrisome to professionals, a change in medication may contribute to a sudden shift in energy from a depressed state, which would elevate a person's risk for a suicide attempt in now having the energy to follow through on making that attempt.

Trainer Tip: Ask about your client's experience with new medications if applicable. Revisit their suicidal scaling of intent after hospitalization. Get them into an appointment slot as close to hospital discharge as possible to reduce their risk of attempting suicide.

Marlena

Marlena reported she wasn't getting quality sleep. She described intense rumination and anxiety that lasted through the night into the early hours of each morning, which was causing a decline in performance at work and in her ability to be mentally present for her daughter. Although she'd had suicidal thoughts for the past eight years, she had no other suicidal behaviors. The only formal diagnosis she reported at intake was anxiety, which was congruent with the rumination and sleep disruption she described in starting therapy.

Rena

Rena was forthcoming about all of her hospitalizations and mental health diagnoses from her previous therapist of two years, which included Post-Traumatic Stress Disorder (PTSD) and Generalized Anxiety Disorder (GAD). Rena had two suicide attempts on record since her teen years, with only one resulting in hospitalization for three days. In her candid style, Rena was quick to name that her means of dying by suicide would involve medication (matching her previous attempts) since she had access to some for her ongoing medical care. She denied access to any firearms and didn't indicate that a gun would be a means for her at present or in the future because she'd always envisioned dying by taking pills, falling asleep, and not waking up.

Tillie

Tillie's distress was evident, as well as her symptoms of elevated anxiety and depression in response to the news of her parents' pending divorce. Her previous self-harm reflected a need to express her internal pain, and she had denied that those previous behaviors were connected to suicide. Tillie reported that an added conflict with her best friend wasn't helping her cope in the present; instead it appeared to be adding to her thought spiral and her urges to resume self-harm due to intense feelings of self-hatred. Tillie continued to voice that she was a burden on her parents and that it would be easier on family and friends if she were gone.

E Is for Engage   **5**

WE'VE ASKED ABOUT SUICIDE and have listened for various risk factors to better understand a client's connection to suicide. Next up, there are two other aspects to engage a client in: stressors and protective factors. Let's explore how each has the potential to increase or decrease risks for suicide.

Stressors

Even though symptoms, mental health diagnoses, and suicide history may all be contributing factors for a particular client, it doesn't mean that they will automatically be at risk for suicide. Sometimes suicide becomes a possibility when stressors are added to the mix in ways that contribute to thoughts and feelings of being overwhelmed and wanting to give up—stressors like

- job loss,
- homelessness,
- relationship end or divorce,
- financial loss or stress,
- failing school,
- relational conflict,
- legal issues,
- grief and loss,
- discrimination and rejection, and
- relocation.

It makes me think of the Holmes–Rahe Stress Inventory, which implies the more stressors a person has experienced in their lifetime, the more likely they are to have a health breakdown, including the possibility of a mental health challenge as a result (American Institute of Stress 2022). Although there isn't a cause-and-effect relationship between stressors and suicide, it's completely human to expect that any added stressor may be met with a "last straw" response, pushing someone to the edge where suicide becomes an option.

Trainer Tip: Inviting clients to speak to all the stressors that are going on in their lives can be eye-opening. Be sure to listen for hopelessness and helplessness as they connect to suicide risk.

Burden

Burdensomeness has been a part of the suicide equation for decades. It can sound like Tillie saying, "they'd be better off without me." Or a phrase like, "they wouldn't notice if I was gone." A feeling of burdensomeness can reinforce a person's belief that things would improve if they weren't alive, contributing to a dangerous assumption that loss survivors like friends, family, and children would have a better life without them in it. I can't help but have the number 135 pop into my head when engaging clients around the thought of being a burden. According to a study titled "How Many People Are Exposed to Suicide? Not Six" (Cerel et al. 2018), 135 is the minimum number of people impacted by each death by suicide. That's just the minimum! The numbers of people impacted can only increase from there and implies that death by suicide ripples out within families and communities, leaving its mark on countless others.

Trainer Tip: Have you ever felt like a burden on your family? How so? Explicitly asking about burdensomeness is recommended because of its strong ties to Thomas Joiner's Capacity for Suicide (2005, p. 138), which we discuss further in this chapter.

Isolation

Is isolation a factor for your client? To feel disconnected from supports or alone in their struggle could add risk for suicide. Is isolation preventing access to resources? Isolation is one of the factors suicide prevention specialists are researching in rural and mountain communities with higher suicide rates because of the limited access to resources that could help.

Trainer Tip: Asking a client how connected or disconnected they feel to others is one way to explore feelings of isolation. I like Lisa Compton's zipper screening

(Compton & Patterson 2023), where solidly connected and fulfilling relationships are represented by a fully zipped zipper, somewhat connected is partially zipped, and lonely with no connection is an open zipper where the two sides aren't touching.

Capacity to Complete Suicide (Dr. Thomas Joiner's Work)

In your mind's eye, picture a Venn diagram of three circles intersecting. In one circle: isolation; in the second circle: burdensomeness; in the third circle: fearlessness. Dr. Thomas Joiner (2005) describes how when these three things are all present, a person has the capacity for suicide. All of us are built with a self-preservation switch that keeps us from harm, like pulling back from a hot stove or getting nervous at a cliff's edge. But Dr. Joiner would describe that if isolation, burdensomeness, and fearlessness are all present, that switch can get turned off, making suicide more possible.

Trainer Tip: Ask about your client's experiences with fear. "Have you ever been in a situation where you felt fearless? What are you afraid of? Are you afraid of pain or death? Why or why not?" Clients who have jobs or experiences that have put them in repeated, fearful situations where they had to adapt to do their jobs (think police, EMTs, firefighters, and military) will exhibit higher levels of fearlessness than others.

Technology Use

Although technology is advancing at a rate faster than we can successfully study it, there is research by Dr. Jean Twenge (2017) that indicates increased risk for suicide based on a certain number of hours of social media use. How many hours could that be? Dr. Twenge (2017) reports that three (3) or more hours of social media per day increases risk for suicide. Why? There are several factors to consider:

- Comparison to others: what's wrong with me, everyone looks so happy/put together/successful/accomplished.
- Sleep disruption: where am I attempting to fit in social media use? Is it in the early morning hours or late into the night when I should be sleeping?
- Cyberbullying: am I experiencing negative and/or hostile interactions with others online? Is this impacting my mood and self-worth?

Trainer Tip: Ask, on average, how many hours per day your client uses social media. What emotional response do they have to social media? Do they notice a change in mood after social media use? Invite them to share on how social media serves them and/or hurts them.

Protective Factors

As we hold space for the heavy load of various stressors, it's also important to engage clients as to what's keeping them alive. I've outright asked this question as something like, "thank you for naming what's making suicide possible for you. I'm curious, what's keeping you alive?" We can continue to model confidence talking about a client's suicide experience by asking the question of protective factors this way. There are two important pieces to emphasize about protective factors for suicide: (1) quantity over quality and (2) the client decides what are and are not protective factors.

Quantity Over Quality

The more protective factors the better. We aren't looking for one particular protective factor to keep someone alive; we are looking for as many things as possible. If it was just one protective factor, imagine the suicidal crisis that would result if that protective factor wasn't an option anymore. Like Marlena, who had named that her daughter was the one reason she was staying alive. Can you imagine what would happen if they had a falling out or if her daughter decided to go live with her dad? Or my nightly caller on the crisis line between undergrad and grad school, who'd call in every night to talk about his suicidal thoughts. He had plans, means, and intent, which made everyone at the call center very nervous. Yet when asked what was keeping him alive, he said it was his dog because no one would be left to take care of his dog if the caller died. It was our job at the hotline to help the caller explore other possible protective factors while embracing the one he had currently, all while praying that nothing happened to his pet.

Client Decides

Which leads us to the second important piece of protective factors: the client gets to decide what is and is not a protective factor. It's based on their values and what's important to them. Please don't make the mistake of suggesting children, family, or partners as protective factors because maybe they don't feel like protective factors to this person, and the suggestion could result in a pain or shame response for your client instead. If a client is struggling to identify protective factors, have them float back to an earlier time in their life where things felt slightly better. What was present then that could be recreated now? Was there a hobby or connection then that can be reignited now?

Although each list of protective factors is unique to each client, the following are some ideas of what clients might say are keeping them alive.

Internal protective factors:

- Fear of pain
- Fear of death
- Fear of messing up a suicide attempt and surviving
- Fear of religious or spiritual scrutiny
- Hope that something better is coming next week/month/year

External protective factors:

- Family
- Friends
- Partners
- Pets
- Children
- Unfinished business
- Future plans (e.g., vacation, time off coming up)
- Worry or guilt about how their death impacts a loved one (e.g., my mom would be devastated)

Trainer Tip: Once a client identifies their protective factors, continue to monitor with them that nothing shifts with those protective factors that would elevate suicide risk (e.g., loss of protective relationship, loss of pet, etc.).

Tillie

Tillie's disclosures had a strong flavor of burdensomeness to them. She was convincing herself in front of my eyes that she didn't deserve to be alive and that she was a bad person. She had identified current stressors as the fight with her best friend that felt more like a breakup in how emotionally painful it was for her, in addition to her parents' divorce. She was clearly overwhelmed and hurting. When asked what was keeping Tillie alive, she named her cat, softball, and an upcoming art show at her school that she didn't want to miss in having a piece of her art featured.

Marlena

Marlena was clear that her daughter was keeping her alive. When explored further, she confirmed that she still had curiosity about starting her own business, especially in having finished her degree recently with possible new opportunities right around the corner. Marlena felt isolated in not having a ton of positive supports in her life, some of which was the result of former abusive relationships that prevented her from spending time with friends. One of our therapy sessions for this newly single parent was dedicated to exploring her interests and possible opportunities to meet people while doing things she enjoyed.

Rena

Rena had a positive support system in her spouse and church community. She didn't feel isolated, but often felt lonely in having to estrange from both her mother and her siblings in response to abuse. Rena recognized that scrolling on social media each day contributed to a shift in mood, usually to a more anxious or depressed state. Part of our work together was redirecting her focus to more pleasurable pursuits that also currently served as protective factors, such as her love of baking and nature photography.

R Is for Respond

6

THE HOPE AT THIS STAGE of a formal suicide assessment is that you feel that you have a fuller picture of your client's suicide story. You've leaned in, you've listened, and you've asked thoughtful questions. The next step is to conceptualize your client's level of risk, which at this time means they land into one of the following categories:

- high risk,
- moderate risk, or
- low risk.

What does each of these designations actually mean? Well as you can imagine, it can feel problematic to place everyone into one of these boxes. It's a narrow view of a person's experience with suicide, to say the least. Yet it's the only option we have right now as mental health professionals, until something better comes along that feels more representative of a person's unique suicide story.

High Risk
High risk as a designation is pretty straightforward in that it speaks to a risk level that indicates immediate action or intervention is needed. My best example of this is when everything and anything can feel like a weapon to attempt suicide. If your client can pick up any object in an attempt to harm themselves, it's pretty telling that there is acute risk that needs to be addressed. If a person has a plan, means, and intent, they can be seen as high risk. Responses to high risk may mean calling 9-1-1, invoking a

mandatory hold as a licensed professional, or asking a loved one to take the client to the hospital.

Moderate Risk

Of the three categories, this one is most challenging for mental health professionals, mainly because something can move a person to high risk, or reduce their risk and move them to the low-risk category. Like my frequent caller to the crisis line, for instance. If the protective factor of his dog were eliminated because the dog died, he'd be immediately placed in the acute, high-risk category in having nothing left keeping him alive. Or maybe moderate risk is like Marlena, who has a couple of protective factors and is interested in expanding upon those, but the relationship with her daughter will dictate her level of risk in being her most important protective factor. If they fight, will Marlena escalate into high risk in feeling that she's lost her daughter and wants to cease living? If they remain close and connected, can she be categorized as low risk with chronic suicidality?

Low Risk

Probably the most perplexing of the three categories, the low-risk designation currently houses 12 million people who've had a suicidal thought (Freedenthal 2023). Surprise! If you have ever had the unbidden image of driving along a windy road and imagined driving off the side of cliff, you are one of the 12 million. If you've ever watched the movie *It's a Wonderful Life* and wondered what life would be like if you weren't in it, you are part of the 12 million. Some of these folks had a suicidal thought decades ago and never again. Yet they are currently listed as low risk for suicide based on that experience. Wild, I know. Folks with suicidal thoughts with no means, plan, or intent fall into the low-risk category as well. What's the right response for these folks? It may be as simple as providing resources like the 9-8-8 number, the text line, the chat line, and locations of crisis stabilization units (CSU) specializing in responding to mental health crises in their area. Unless they have something change in regard to diagnoses, symptoms, or stressors that makes things worse, there is most likely minimal intervention needed on behalf of the mental health professional.

Acute Versus Chronic

I've mentioned the word *acute* when describing high risk above. Acute serves the same purpose in mental health care as in medical care, implying immediate response and action is needed to save a life. Chronic, on the other hand, indicates a persistent state of being, in this case, constant or steady suicidal thoughts. As Frank King, mental health comedian and TEDx speaker would say, "suicide is always on the menu." Folks with chronic suicidality are living with suicidal thoughts day to day. The thoughts may be running in the background in ways that don't fully disrupt their lives. For some clients, this doesn't cause them any distress; in fact, it might bring them comfort to have suicide remain an option. Comforting to know that suicide is a choice if things don't improve, meaning that they can still escape pain if needed. Therefore chronic suicidality may mean repeated or persistent suicidal thoughts, although plans, means, or intent remain absent.

Action Steps

So as you can imagine, our action steps will look different for a client found to be at high risk for suicide versus someone categorized as low risk for suicide. Our response as professional helpers will look equally different for someone with acute suicidal thoughts versus someone with chronic suicidal thoughts. If acute means repeated, intense thoughts that are difficult to control and cause the person experiencing them measurable distress, chronic can mean repeated suicidal thoughts in the background with limited distress. Our response to each will need to look different when honoring these two experiences. Where acute, high, or moderate risk may be about accessing higher levels of care, chronic suicidality is best approached from a place of resourcing. Resourcing means helping the client continue to build quality coping skills to manage stressors and in support of emotion regulation, in addition to maintaining a positive therapeutic relationship. Maintaining the quality therapeutic relationship also means holding space for the comfort that suicide remaining an option can bring your client. To ask someone who has experienced suicidal thoughts for months or years to remove suicide as an option is a sure way to encourage a relationship rupture in therapy due to the person not feeling seen or understood. By leaning into the person's experience with suicide and embracing space for their suicide story, we can build trust where our client can name if something shifts in their experience with suicidal thoughts, resulting in additional assessment and exploration of action steps as needed.

Safety Planning

Verbal contracts of the 1980s and 1990s have been replaced with safety planning (Joiner, 2005, p. 212). Meant to be an empowerment tool to support a client's coping during intense moments of mental health distress or suicidal thought, a safety plan is best received when it is crafted collaboratively between therapist and client.

Adapted from Stanley and Brown (2008), a suicide safety plan has the following components:

1. baseline wellness,
2. warning signs and triggers,
3. personal and professional supports,
4. make the environment safe, and
5. action plan.

Baseline Wellness

Meant to be a question to ease a client into safety planning, the baseline wellness question is an invitation for the client to sit in self-awareness. What does it look like when I'm well? What does it look like when I'm unwell? Although the responses will be unique to your client, some possible examples of what you may hear from various clients are found in Table 6.1.

Warning Signs and Triggers

Warning signs are the internal signs that things are declining. What can your client name that happens to them? Can they identify when they cry more easily? Snap at others? Feel restless or agitated? Experience anxiety or fatigue? Numb out or dissociate? Hand in hand with the internal experience a client notices for themselves is the external experience of feeling triggered. Triggers may be things like conflict with a partner, failing something, hearing the phrase, "we need to talk," shouting or fighting, or

Table 6.1.

When I'm Well	When I'm Unwell
I'm animated.	I have limited facial expression.
I have energy.	I'm tired and fatigued.
I take my medication.	I don't take my medication.
I sleep okay.	I don't sleep well or regularly.
I'm in control of my emotions.	I have a short fuse.
I'm regulated.	I snap easily at others.
I'm on time.	I'm late to things.
I'm social.	I cancel or ghost people.
I have an appetite.	I don't eat regularly.

a trauma anniversary. I can't tell you how many clients I've served over the years who come in for one session saying they don't know why they feel so sad or low. My first question in my empathetic response is always, "Is there something significant about this date, month, or season?" Nine times out of 10, they have a trauma anniversary that they've blocked from their mind, but their body remembers.

Personal and Professional Supports

Professional supports remain a pretty easy section to complete on a safety plan with a client. It encompasses resources like 9-8-8, the text line, the chat line, you as their mental health professional, their medical doctor, and more. As we named previously, the question about personal supports can be sort of tricky for folks who don't feel that they have many people in their life who care about them. This is your chance to try out the who-can-provide-a-healthy-distraction question (see Chapter 4)! Does this reframing help them put some people on their list as personal supports because the stakes don't feel so high in not having to disclose suicide?

Make the Environment Safe

Exactly as it sounds, this section of a safety plan is all about what steps can be taken to improve physical and emotional safety within the client's environment. Is it about securing weapons, locking up pills, removing a gun from the home, or increasing supervision so they aren't left alone? Is it a matter of removing razors and scissors, locking up alcohol, or bunking with a buddy until the crisis lightens? Explore this aspect fully with your client to see what might be beneficial to increasing their safety.

Action Plan

Recognized as the most customized part of a safety plan for each client, what action steps can your client take in support of their own safety? Similar to a harm reduction model (Marlatt 1996), what can your client try first, second, and third to keep themselves safe? It reminds me of imagery of panic attacks being mapped on a bell curve. Although the experience of a panic attack is unpleasant and scary for most people, the most intense part—the top of the bell curve—tends to last 15–60 seconds (Kessler et al., 2006). So when working with panic disorder, many professionals will explore what coping skills could work for a client in that critical window of time. When it comes to suicide, what can the client embrace in their own coping kit to make it through the most intense part of their suicide experience? Can they call 9-8-8, call a friend, take a walk, listen to music, pet their cat, exercise, do breath work, journal, meditate, cry, clean, and more?

Safety planning is a tool that can be used for more than just suicide. It can be used for domestic violence, family conflict, relapse prevention within substance treatment, and to reduce self-harm behaviors. What makes it most successful is the collaboration with the client. If the client isn't invested in the safety plan, why would they use it? I recall a teenage client I'd started working with who had a safety plan written as he was discharged from residential treatment. To the question of what coping skills he'd like to use, he'd written "I'll use my coping skills." Clearly the safety plan at that time for this client was not helpful, and his response indicated a lack of buy-in to use it since it was unclear what skills he'd actually try. Letting clients know that the safety plan can be revised as many times as needed as they try different coping skills can also take the pressure off. If they try a skill this week and find it didn't provide relief, what can be added instead that feels worth trying next time?

Marlena

Marlena clearly landed in the chronic suicidality category when starting therapy. She had managed suicidal thoughts for the last eight years on her own and was building in more protective factors while seeking regular therapy to see if things could change for the better. Her level of risk at that time was somewhere between low and moderate based on the number and quality of interactions with her daughter. Marlena consented to building a safety plan together for the darker moments that occurred for her in the late hours of the night, when rumination and lack of sleep appeared to turn the volume up on her suicidal thoughts. Her action plan included (1) calling a friend who was also a night owl known to be awake at 3:00 a.m., (2) turning on music, (3) trying a muscle relaxation exercise to see if it could help her fall sleep, and (4) researching events in her area that might be worth checking out in the next few weeks for something to look forward to, as well as supporting her goal of increased social connections.

Rena

Rena also had frequent suicidal thoughts, although not chronic in that they weren't with her more days than not. Her suicidal thoughts got louder after fights with her spouse, which were happening more frequently lately as they both stressed about their efforts to get pregnant. Rena liked the idea of scaling her suicidal thoughts as part of her therapeutic check-in, including naming what percentage of her wanted to live versus die, and a number 1–10 that indicated her intent to die (see Chapter 3). Rena was diligent about recording her numbers each morning and night, as well as after conflict with her spouse to see if there was any pattern to her thoughts of suicide. She was open to having a safety plan for the moments where her numbers crept up to over 50% wanting to die, or when her intent was over 7. Rena's safety plan included (1) taking a walk to take pictures outside, (2) calling her best friend who worked from home, and (3) petting and hugging her dog.

Tillie

In my efforts to show Tillie that therapy was a safe place to discuss her suicidal thoughts, she decided to disclose that she had in fact self-harmed earlier in the day connected to those suicidal thoughts. She also admitted to having a plan to kill herself, which involved throwing herself off the overpass near the office with closer to 8 out of 10 intent (she'd previously reported 7 at the start of the session). Because Tillie had accessible means, a lethal plan, and was showing risk in the form of feelings of being a burden, current self-harm, and serious intention to follow through on her plans, her suicide risk was determined to be high. In an effort to not leave Tillie alone unsupervised, I explained to her the next steps of getting her more support, including texting her mom to enter the therapy room from the waiting room outside. Tillie's mom agreed to take her to the hospital, where Tillie was admitted for 72 hours due to her being seen as a danger to herself.

T Is for Tasks

7

ALTHOUGH THIS LAST PIECE of our ALERT acronym is simple, it's equally important to you as the clinician assessing for suicide with your client as any other piece of the ALERT acronym. Perhaps your graduate education also drilled into you the phrase: *document it or it didn't happen!* Meant to emphasize the importance of a paper trail, it actually serves more than the traditional (and oftentimes irritating) cover-your-ass purpose reiterated in professional programs. I agree that it's best-practice to have a formal suicide assessment document filled out, preferably with the client present. Fortunately many of the most popular suicide assessments can be printed or completed digitally, which allows for this collaboration without leaving a client in suicidal crisis unsupervised. Let's take a look at other tasks related to professional documentation below as part of T for Tasks.

Purposes of suicide assessment documentation:

1. Capturing critical incidents
2. Supporting supervision and consultation
3. Collaborating on higher levels of care
4. Providing a client copy for their records

Capturing Critical Incidents

Many professionals would place suicidal thoughts in clients under the textbook definition of a critical incident. By nature, a critical incident requires a professional response to support safety. So completing a formal suicidal assessment may be the first piece to our tasks as therapists, with a second piece being a critical incident form to complete, especially if you are an unlicensed therapist under supervision, work for a clinic or group practice, or report to an agency. Most critical incident forms include a section on (1) what happened, (2) the response, (3) supervisor or consultant recommen-dations, and (4) outcomes. Whereas a suicide assessment can be completed in real time with a client, the critical incident form may be a task for after the fact based on it being a snapshot of events and responses to those events to successfully document safety concerns.

Supporting Supervision and Consultation

As indicated with critical incidents, a paper trail may be required if you are under the supervision of a licensed therapist or seek support from a profes-sional consultant or colleague. Supervision requires a supervisee to follow the recommendations of their supervisor as the license-holder and leader, whereas a professional consultation allows the consultee to take or leave any advice or recommendations received by their consultant as they see fit. Regardless of the professional encounter being supervision or consultation, a document capturing what was discussed is expected, and can be stream-lined when completed in conjunction with a formal suicide assessment.

Collaborating on Higher Levels of Care

Another benefit of completing a formal suicide assessment document in real time with your clients is the ability to send a copy with a client for possible collaboration and access to a higher level of care. It's not uncom-mon for a client to meet risk criteria, be sent to a hospital, and wait 3–4 hours for another crisis evaluation, only to minimize their suicidal thoughts with that evaluator in wanting to go home. It's a human response to feel scared and frustrated while idling in an emergency room. So sending a copy of your suicide assessment can serve two purposes when it comes to a higher level of care: (1) it can support the client not having to repeat themselves when another provider is assessing them, and (2) it can indicate your involvement as their mental health professional and the assessment you've already done to justify why they are being evaluated further for higher levels of care. The hope is that, because the hospital staff knows you exist, they will also feel inclined to call you to get your clinical take on things and/or follow up with you on the outcome of their assessment with your client.

Trainer Tip: Put your name, credentials, relationship to the client, and phone number at the top of the copy of your suicide assessment so hospital staff know to call you with updates on your client.

Providing a Client Copy for Their Records

A final justification for documenting your suicide assessment as a valuable and worthwhile task is that it provides the paper trail a client and/or their family may need to access services or get insurance to pay for those services. I've had parents request records for the sole reason of presenting a case to their private insurance to pay for residential or intensive outpatient treatment, with the hopes that it would be life-saving for their child. Although this document isn't confidential because of its connection to client safety, I've always explained to clients what the purpose of sharing a copy is so that they may feel reassured that my efforts are to help and not stigmatize or hurt them further with these documents. Giving a client a copy of their own assessment invites them to ask questions or request corrections to information written, which gives them some autonomy in a crisis where they may feel they have limited or no say in what happens next.

So what do we document as part of our tasks? I've mentioned the importance of a formal suicide assessment as part of your paper trail. You may also have a critical incident report, consultation record, or progress note to bill for your time with the client while in crisis if your insurance contract allows or if crisis management is a service outlined in your private pay fee agreement. In order to avoid feeling repetitive, I oftentimes suggest to my students that they capture the most vital aspects of their suicide assessment in a therapy note, to include the following:

1. level of risk including risk factors,
2. steps taken, and
3. outcomes.

So for Tillie as our current high-risk example, a progress note might look something like this:

Client was found to be at high risk for suicide due to reports of recent self-harm, suicidal thoughts, plans, means, and intent as well as risk factors of burdensomeness, relational conflict, and elevated stressors with minimal protective factors reported by client. Client was formally assessed for suicide (see included assessment) and was informed of next steps by this therapist due to being found at high risk. Mother verbally agreed to take client to (name) hospital. Outcomes to follow.

Since it can take several hours for a formal assessment at a hospital to be completed, your outcome section may be a chart note once you receive additional information.

Chart note example:

Received phone call from Dr. Miller at (name) hospital, who identified himself as the assessor for client suicide. Dr. Miller reports client met criteria for a 72-hour hold and would remain at (name) hospital for the duration. Agreement to coordinate discharge plan for resumption of mental health outpatient therapy as appropriate.

An additional task for Tillie may be updating her safety plan upon resumption of care. A different task may be a discharge summary if a client is referred to a higher level of care or is in the care of another provider or service for a longer duration. Your tasks will continue to be heavily focused on documentation in support of your client, which is why it remains an important step in your clinical process with suicide.

Tillie

Upon Tillie's discharge from a 72-hour hold, my tasks included ongoing communication with her mom and dad, safety planning with parents' verbal consent to support the current plan, seeking a family referral for Tillie, her mom, and her dad to process the divorce, and assessing my current relationship with Tillie after hospitalization. Tillie was understandably cautious at first in our next session, her eyes half hidden under her choppy self-inflicted bangs as she looked at me. I invited her to share what the experience had been like, and Tillie expressed her anger at the process and relief to be home. In recognizing my openness to receive her feedback about the suicide assessment process, Tillie grounded herself in exploring what she needed to feel better going forward, while also focusing on what would prevent hospitalization for herself in the future.

Marlena

Tasks for Marlena looked different since we weren't doing a formal suicide assessment in response to her low risk factors. She was maintaining a level of positive coping that she disclosed in weekly individual therapy, and reported that she was using her safety plan in the early hours of the morning when needed. My concern was in Marlena getting less than four hours of sleep a night, a deficit that appeared to be impacting her cognitive functioning. One of my tasks in working with Marlena was to continue to assess her sleep hygiene and to explore the possibility of a sleep study through her primary care physician. Marlena was in agreement to meeting with her doctor to explore her bloodwork to rule out any other medical factors that could be disrupting her sleep, and was prepared to ask for the sleep study referral at that appointment.

Rena

Although Rena's numbers (percentage wanting to live versus percentage wanting to die and her level of intent with dying by suicide) continued to fluctuate, she was forthcoming about sharing her numbers weekly with me. Our tasks remained (1) reducing her stress levels, and (2) increasing her coping skills, all while monitoring her current moderate suicide risk due to her suicide attempt history and ongoing conflict with her spouse as a primary trigger for spiraling out of her safety zone. We agreed to meet twice some weeks when her numbers appeared too high for comfort, with her asking for additional support as she neared another menstrual cycle to see if she was pregnant.

Tragedy Strikes, But for Whom?   8

Marlena

Marlena came into my office for our scheduled session looking different in presentation. Her movements were abrupt, she was absent of color, both in her missing accessories and in her face, and her tone was clipped when I retrieved her from the waiting room. She plopped into her preferred chair in a way I hadn't seen before. I started our session by reflecting what I was seeing, including how I could see her fidgeting more than usual, with eye contact that bounced from my face to around the room, and how her posture showed more rigidity than in previous sessions. I also internally noted how her energy seemed more intense and how she clutched her purse on her lap, which could be interpreted as a barrier or shield. Something had changed. After naming what I was seeing, I invited her to share. She disclosed that she and her daughter had had a big fight and how her daughter had threatened to go live with her dad. Marlena's response, out of hurt and anger, had been to encourage her daughter to go.

Rena

It had been a couple weeks since Rena found out she was pregnant. She had been excited and overwhelmed by various emotions, and her spouse had responded favorably by being more attentive and loving at the news of her pregnancy. When Rena came in for her scheduled appointment, she looked ill. She was pale with dark circles under her golden-colored eyes, and she appeared smaller, as I watched her curl in on herself with hands pressed gently to her torso. As soon as the door was closed, she started to cry. "I've lost the baby," she said, collapsing further into herself. "I don't want to keep living."

Tillie

Our most recent session had Tillie looking the most animated and bubbly than I'd ever seen. It was almost like she was a different person. She shared about starting to talk with her closest friend again, how she was looking forward to softball practices several nights a week, and how she was adjusting to new medication and alternating between her mom and dad's houses on a set schedule each week. Although her grades had slipped during her depressed state several weeks earlier, she shared that she was working to get her grades back up and had started to dabble in art again.

Each of their stories can ring some warning bells for therapists. Marlena's greatest protective factor—her daughter—was considering living with her dad after a fight with Marlena. Her defensive and hurt response was to lash out and goad her daughter into going, all while pursuing a relationship with a former, abusive ex-boyfriend. Would this be enough to change Marlena's chronic, low risk for suicide to something that felt more moderate or acute? Or Rena, who reported a significant and acute loss of a miscarriage. As mental health professionals, we can expect this to push Rena's numbers up, dialing up her desire to die as well as her intent to die by suicide after she disclosed additional suicidal thoughts in response to this loss.

What about Tillie? Things seemed to be going well on the surface, but she was also super animated and bubbly, possibly euphoric in her presentation. For some clients, this can be a warning sign that they've made a decision to die and are feeling elated or at peace with the decision. Or how about the change in medication adding risk in coming out of a depressive episode? How would you explore these possibilities with Tillie to rule out a decision of suicide as a possible reason for her improved mood, rather than adjustment, medication, and stabilization of her protective factors as the cause for her happier state?

When Folks Are Spiraling

I received a cryptic text from Marlena at two in the morning. Her daughter had packed her bags and left after another fight, and Marlena was spiraling. I didn't get the text until I woke up hours later.

Tillie's mom called me to share she'd found a suicide note in Tillie's room when she was cleaning and putting away laundry. Tillie's mom was unsure when it was written, and asked for support due to worrying that Tillie might be at risk of suicide again.

Rena texted me to share her husband was rushed to the hospital last night after a severe allergic reaction to a medication he had started taking, and had died of complications. I immediately tried to call her after reading her message, but she didn't answer the phone.

Tillie made it to our appointment that week, and shared her numbers had remained 50/50 but her intent to die had fluctuated on her new medication, with the highest number being 8. She also shared that she was stressed she wouldn't be able to play at her softball game that week because of her low grades, which made her look less happy and more disheartened in our latest session. When asked about the suicide note, Tillie shared that she wrote it in a low moment rather than engaging in self-harm. She reported it helped her express her pain without cutting or scratching herself.

Marlena responded to my outreach hours later after she reported she finally got some sleep. She didn't share a ton of information on the phone but confirmed her appointment for later in the week. When she didn't show up in the waiting room, I called her, with no answer. I started the process of outreaching her in multiple ways, wondering if I needed to call in a welfare check if she didn't respond.

Rena asked for a phone session that week, having to plan her husband's memorial. She was tearful and overwhelmed on the phone, attempting to bear both the grief of her miscarriage with the sudden death of her spouse. Her numbers were higher, but she claimed she was focused on getting her husband's affairs in order to do right by him, rather than being focused on dying, herself.

Receiving Tragic News

You are probably wondering who died by suicide in my professional story. Tillie, Rena, or Marlena? Now comes the reveal. She had told me the suicidal thoughts were getting louder and she was tired of fighting. She had also told me that she had a plan and a timeline, but that she wouldn't share any of it with me out of fear of hospitalization. It felt like she'd tied my hands, and so I sought consultation. It was reassuring to hear from another professional that her engagement with me was a strength—that perhaps sharing plans of dying brought this client some comfort. It was also helpful to me to receive confirmation from my consultant that hospitalizing my client based on worry alone wasn't going to work. I leaned into the knowing that we were still actively talking about things, and she continued to share her numbers daily to let me know where she was at in her suicide story.

Then a typical Colorado spring snowstorm hit, the texts stopped, and her phone was off when I called. My gut sank as my heartbeat pounded loudly in my head. I'd put in a welfare check after 24 hours of hoping she'd get back to me, waiting for the apology that she'd dropped her phone and had to get a new one. That had to be the explanation, right? Well, that didn't happen, so I waited to see what the police could tell me after visiting her home on a welfare check. My heart said it was too late, that she'd already died by suicide. I didn't have an emergency contact on file to call. Her phone remained off and went straight to voicemail after multiple attempts to reach her.

Her loss had been significant, leaving her irrevocably changed, and it had remained a focus of our therapy for good reason, bringing suicide closer to the surface as a means of escape more and more each week in our work together. I was working from home to avoid driving in the snow when the police called me back and said they had knocked on the door, no one had answered, so they had left. I was enraged when I hung up the phone. Really, that was it? *Nothing else could be done?* This was quickly followed by a flood of tears as I was more and more certain she was dead.

The second call came the next day, a voicemail from a woman identifying herself as a friend. *Rena had died by suicide.* This friend had found her in her apartment after using her spare key to get inside and was calling all the people Rena had left on a list, having asked her friend in writing to notify them of Rena's death. I called the friend back, having heard of her from Rena as someone who had helped Rena with her husband's funeral plans and who had been grounding for Rena in this last month's rollercoaster ride of grief. This friend had heard Rena with me on the phone several times before Rena sat in her car for privacy, and she had encouraged Rena to continue therapy during this difficult time. I felt for her friend, not knowing what would happen in the call. The friend shared her own anguish, grief, and sadness in having found Rena dead and, on top of that, having discovered her several days later in her room. My imagination filled in the ghastly details as I held space for this poor woman who had lost a friend. It was only after ending the call with Rena's friend that I allowed myself to feel that loss too, sobbing and calling my closest colleagues in the hopes of comfort and support.

Part II

HEART

A Clinician's Response to Suicide   9

I T GOES WITHOUT SAYING that the loss of a client to suicide has a significant impact on professional helpers. One study by Hammond indicated that among health care professionals who had experienced both patient suicides and personal suicides, the professionals felt more responsible for the suicides of patients (Weiner 2005). Donna M. James (Weiner 2005) said, "Therapists are likely to be personally wounded when patients kill themselves, this wounding appearing as guilt, shame, or denial." Wounding feels accurate in capturing the profound effect a client death by suicide has on their therapist, with several studies (Weiner 2005) indicating 3–6 months of post-traumatic symptoms in providers as a result. Let's take a look at the experiences of providers from the lens of Alex Castro Croy's (2022) PERMS, which stands for physical, emotional, relational, mental, and spiritual domains of self.

Physical

- Muscle tension, aches, spasms
- Sleep disruption
- Tension headaches
- Muscle spasms
- Elevated startle response
- Fear
- Fatigue
- Stomach distress
- Loss of appetite

- Weight loss or weight gain
- Eczema
- Inflammation
- Increased tearfulness

Muscle Tension, Aches, Spasms

This could be situational where a professional feels more tense in certain situations or environments, like driving to work, while writing notes, or when talking about their client's suicide. It can also be all-encompassing, resulting in elevated pain and stiffness after sitting or lying down for periods of time. Certain parts of the body may hold more aches, pains, or spasms that, at first glance, don't feel connected to a client loss to suicide.

Sleep Disruption

The culprit of many mental health conditions, sleep disruption after a client suicide could mean nightmares, night terrors, unbidden images of the client or client's death, waking up frequently, or difficulty falling asleep. For many professionals, attempting to fall asleep becomes a vulnerable time when images arrive unwelcome in our minds or we struggle with rumination in not having the same distractions we experience (and rely on) during the day.

Tension Headaches

Similar to muscle tension in other parts of the body, tension headaches can result from many things. Ones to note include a clenched jaw, slouched body posture, and sitting for long periods in front of a computer, such as when we offer telehealth sessions to clients. Is it possible that tension headaches arrive from holding your body a certain way that coveys successful coping or confidence when maybe you are feeling neither successful at coping nor confident after a client suicide? The incongruence and effort to appear to be functioning "normally" could result in tension headaches.

Elevated Startle Response

This can look like jumping at unexpected noises or movement, or flinching when being touched unexpectedly; for some, it signifies a disruption in spatial awareness where they start dropping items, run into doorways or furniture, or describe an overall sense of clumsiness. This can serve as an indicator of stress, or rushing and needing to slow down, or dissociation when running into objects that normally don't pose a problem in our pre-dictable, everyday environment.

Fear

Although fear shows up in other aspects of our functioning, including mentally and relationally regarding client suicide, fear can also show up somatically as rapid heart rate, sweating, nausea, stomach pain, and more. One professional I interviewed who had experienced multiple client suicides within their career reported a metallic taste in their mouth that arrived immediately on the heels of getting the tragic news of their clients' deaths. As we can imagine, any activation of the fight-or-flight response could be part of our body's response to this traumatic event.

Fatigue

A client suicide doesn't always seem to have a clear connection to fatigue, and yet so many of us report deep fatigue in response to this kind of loss. Does fatigue arrive with grief? Does it show up when attempting to func-tion and "push through" our symptoms of distress and loss? Is fatigue the result of overworking and distracting or ruminating on what happened in the months, weeks, days, or hours before our client's death? Fatigue can show up immediately following the loss, as well as weeks or months later, and can be mislabeled as workplace burnout.

Stomach Distress

Our stomachs can tell us a lot about how we are functioning. Even when we look cool and collected on the outside, our stomach can tell a differ-ent story. This may show up as gas and bloating, new sensitivity to foods, nausea, and digestion challenges like constipation or diarrhea.

Loss of Appetite

Due to all the somatic symptoms we've named so far, a loss of appetite may be the natural result. With anxiety, fear, and body aches showing up, it makes sense that a professional may report a loss of appetite. Appetite can also be disrupted by the emotional toll of the client loss to suicide, such as intense guilt and shame dictating what we eat, when we eat, and why we eat.

Weight Loss or Weight Gain

Based on the immense stress we are experiencing in our bodies in response to the loss of a client to suicide, we can experience weight loss or weight gain. If there's a loss of appetite, does this contribute to the body's response of holding onto calories and storing them as fat cells? Does a professional lose weight rapidly if they aren't eating regularly? It may also be possible that a professional develops disordered eating behaviors out of a desire for a sense of control; that could result in weight loss or weight gain as well.

Eczema

Speaking of stress responses in the body, an increase in eczema can be another indicator as a professional attempts to cope with their client's suicide. With the skin being the biggest organ of the human body, it makes sense that skin would show us the toll of stress through increased outbreaks of eczema, hives, or acne, as just a few examples.

Inflammation

Inflammation doesn't restrict itself to just the skin, either. Inflammation can also mean stomach distress, puffiness, swollen limbs, water retention, and hair loss. Similar to chronic burnout, inflammation can be linked to autoimmune conditions and flare-ups that can feel difficult to manage on top of grief and loss with a client suicide.

Increased Tearfulness

Lastly, bringing us from physical symptoms to our emotional symptoms checklist is increased tearfulness. Maybe you know yourself well and recognize what makes you cry. Maybe you've always been able to cry easily. But perhaps you feel like the tears are lingering just below the surface, where crying happens more frequently and without the same level of control you once felt in managing tears well. This can look like getting teary eyed with clients when you never have before; crying more easily at movies, shows, and commercials; or feeling quick to cry in response to elevated emotions, such as happiness, anger, and sadness.

Emotional

- Shame
- Guilt

- Self-blame
- Accepting responsibility
- Questioning competency
- Fear about licensing board discipline
- Worry about family accusations or a pending lawsuit
- Anxiety
- Unbidden images
- Rumination
- Hypervigilance
- Quick to cry
- Irritability

Shame

Probably the most common emotional response a professional can have when experiencing a client suicide, shame feels dangerous. It shows up frequently and reinforces internal beliefs of responsibility and being at fault. It can sound like, "how could I not see this coming? I'm a bad therapist. I can't keep people safe. I should quit. People can't trust me to keep them safe." What makes this worse is when we already have these beliefs, and our colleagues' responses reinforce them by indicating blame or negligence on our part as the therapist working with the client who has died by suicide. Chapter 12 offers more thoughts on how community members can hurt or help.

Guilt

Where shame says "I'm wrong," guilt says "I did something wrong." Guilt can show up as the urge to look back through our notes to see if we did something wrong that would be tied to our client dying. It's an urge to confirm guilt or innocence. To hold our breath and only release it when no blame can be found. Guilt is also the psychological autopsy or review of your entire case file immediately after your client's death, an experience your leadership team can demand hours into your shock or trauma response. We can feel guilty for all sorts of reasons, including worries of missing something, questioning if we colluded in their death, or worrying that we didn't fight hard enough to keep our client(s) alive—that is, if we knew suicide was a part of their experience. If we feel blindsided by their death by suicide, the guilt can sound even louder as it demands why we, as professionals, didn't see this coming. Similar to shame, guilt hurts and can do a lot of damage to our professional competence and confidence in our abilities. More can be found on professional competence and confidence in Chapter 11.

Self-Blame

If we experience guilt and shame and find evidence that we could have done something more, or something different, self-blame gets added to the mix. It sounds like, "this is my fault. I should have done more. I should have hospitalized them. I should have asked them about suicide. I should have known." Lots of "shouldas" on this self-blame train. This feeds into a decline in therapist confidence and feelings of limited competence within the field, which only serves to add to the stigma of having a client die by suicide. Additionally, it can reinforce the illusion that client suicide isn't happening to other professionals; it's only happening to us because of our own negligence.

Accepting Responsibility

"It's my fault they died." If we absorb the guilt, shame, and self-blame into ourselves and call it our truth, we are taking responsibility for our client's choice to die by suicide. If that doesn't raise some red flags, read that sentence again. How can it be our responsibility to keep another person alive? How does this work against a client's right to autonomy? Several colleagues I interviewed for this book were fans of Internal Family Systems (IFS), and quoted founder Richard Schwartz, who said of suicide, "their parts determined this was what was best for them" (Schwartz 2023). Accepting responsibility for another person's choices feels like a boundary violation because it is.

Questioning Competency

Interwoven in emotional, relational, and spiritual spheres of our lives, questioning our own competency is a common immediate response to a client death by suicide. It feels magnified by the stories we tell ourselves, as well as the response of our mental health community, which includes leaders and supervisors. Although questioning tends to fade over time through the healing process, the best response colleagues and leaders can give to a clinician whose client has died by suicide is compassion and sharing of their own experience if applicable. Chapter 13 offers more on how this response helps.

Fear About Licensing Board Discipline

It's not uncommon for the first thought after learning of a client death by suicide to be about our professional license being at risk. Fear of being found at fault is a natural response to this type of trauma as professionals attempting to help our clients. I call licensing boards "the big bad wolf" because of how they can make clinicians feel. Identified as the governing body for how we do things ethically in practice, their focus is on quality client care, which sometimes conveys a message of "guilty until proven innocent" when it comes to a professional's actions or a possible grievance investigation for mental health professionals. Fear shows up when we think about the shame of board action, a red mark on our record, or the loss of our professional identity, not to mention the worry of our livelihood being taken from us if our license were to be revoked.

Worry About Family Accusations or a Pending Lawsuit

Following closely on the heels of board action, clinicians can have worries about a client's family's accusations or a lawsuit in response to the family's grief. What if the family accuses us of not doing our job? What if they want to find us at fault for their loved one's death? What if they blame us? Grief responses to suicide of a loved one can include anger, which may be directed toward the therapist as the professional involved and can reinforce mixed messages of it being our "job" to keep people alive.

Anxiety

We know that a client death by suicide is emotional, which means anxiety can be part of our grief response. Anxiety can show up as worry about scrutiny, fault, and responsibility. It can also show up as a hyperfocus on other clients in our practice or anxious anticipation of future suicides. As one colleague described it in their interview with me, "I was constantly wondering who would be next."

Unbidden Images

Something not talked about enough in the aftermath of a client suicide is unbidden images. Images of your client flash before your eyes, unexpected and oftentimes unwanted. If you're lucky, it's just the innocent image of how they looked when you last saw them, such as them smiling on your couch, or walking out the door saying, "see you next week." If you are unlucky in the sense of having a detailed account of their suicide, your mind fills in the blanks of how they looked in death. The images don't even have to be gruesome to be unsettling; it's the fact that they arrive without a sense of control over when, how, and how often they show up in our mind's eye that makes them feel disruptive.

Rumination

Similar to unbidden images, rumination also feels uncontrollable to many professionals. To think and rethink the events of our client's death and the time leading up to their death is natural because it's our brain's attempt at making sense of what happened. We may also find ourselves exploring other scenarios over and over, where one detail is changed that could lead to a different outcome.

Hypervigilance

The same as with any other traumatic event, hypervigilance can be a part of our experience when a client has died by suicide. We've named the elevated startle response as part of the physical domain, whereas hypervigilance from the emotional lens looks like over-asking other clients about thoughts of suicide, remaining hyperaware of any language or disclosures that look linkable to suicidal thought, or feeling on edge when a client describes depression or a decline in well-being where suicide might be more possible. One colleague I interviewed shared how they weren't fully aware of how their hypervigilance was driving their therapeutic work until a client pointed out that they'd just asked about suicidal thoughts the week before, to which the client had responded no, and then the therapist asked them again the next week, leaving the client confused and a little frustrated.

Quick to Cry

We mentioned increased tearfulness in the physical symptoms section, but it's worth categorizing the faster access to tears in the emotional response section as well. Why? Because a trauma response leaves us as professionals feeling raw and tender when holding difficult topics for others. Are we finding ourselves quick to cry at things that didn't seem to activate this level of response before? Are tears more accessible when hearing of someone else's loss to suicide? Tears are showing up for many reasons, with their existence right below the surface making them more difficult to control.

Irritability

A short fuse, or increased irritability, can be a sign of the emotional toll a client suicide is having on us as professionals. Are we finding ourselves easily frustrated with clients? Are we more intolerant of late cancellations and no-shows in our schedule? Are we noticing resentment toward certain clients who feel more taxing on us emotionally? Do we take out our frustrations on our partners or spouses, nitpicking things and exploding about things that didn't previously bother us? Notice how irritability can mask fear and anxiety under a protective shell of anger. Irritability may feel safer at first, but it can have a negative impact on the relational support we require when attempting to heal from a client suicide.

Relational

- Defensiveness
- Avoidance
- Changes in speech
- I'll be blamed.
- I can't share this with anyone.
- My colleagues will judge me.
- My supervisor will fire me.
- My community won't trust me.
- I'll be reported to my licensing board.

Defensiveness

It's hard not to feel defensive when mental health colleagues and community members may intentionally or unintentionally reinforce our feelings of responsibility or blame for our client's death by suicide. This may mean our tone or body language changes, or our response remains cautious with the urge to shut down. It may mean we are quick to anger or irritability. The urge to defend ourselves when worrying about life-altering consequences makes sense, although it makes it that much harder to connect with people who truly want to help us after our client's suicide.

Avoidance

As the result of our internal battle and resulting grief, we may avoid interacting with others after a client suicide. This is especially true when the other person may have said or done something that reinforces our own worries, feels blaming or shaming, or feels dismissive to our experience at this significant point of your grief process. This results in active avoidance, like taking the stairs to avoid running into someone in the elevator, working from home, or screening your calls because you don't want to talk to anyone. There is also passive avoidance, like throwing yourself into being extra busy at work to avoid social commitments, responding "I'm fine" without truly thinking about it, or deflecting by asking someone else about themselves to avoid thinking about your current experience. Avoidance of slowing down to feel or avoidance of sharing those feelings with others can prolong grief and prevent meaningful healing. More on the importance of connecting with others after your client's suicide can be found in Chapter 11.

Changes in Speech

Sometimes lumped in with defensiveness, a change in speech could serve as an indicator of how you are doing with the loss of your client to suicide. It could be that you are talking differently because you *are* feeling defensive. But what about when it's the result of hypervigilance? Or a jadedness meant to protect you from the ever-present alarm that another client suicide is possible? What if your clipped speech is meant to be a shield against interacting too deeply with others? Could it indicate that you are hanging on by a thread and don't want to talk too long, or the tears will come pouring out too? Or perhaps our clipped speech indicates the negative headspace we are in as we grieve? As a professional, changes in speech are connected to cognitive shifts that could create ruptures with other clients and colleagues if messaging feels dismissive, defensive, negative, or cold in our attempts to protect ourselves.

I'll Be Blamed.

A common fear after a client's death by suicide, worries of being blamed make us each show up differently in our relationships. If you aren't avoiding, you may be speaking differently. You could be keeping people at arm's length out of fear of being judged or hurt further. We may elect to stay surface level in our interactions to protect ourselves, pulling back even further from the support that could help us most.

I Can't Share This With Anyone.

With how busy we all are, it can feel almost too easy to avoid sharing the traumatic event of losing a client to suicide. Most of my network (until this book) had no idea about my client suicide as I felt compelled to keep functioning and show up unchanged in other areas of my life. I know I'm not alone in my effort to keep chugging along after my client's death, although the true question is, *at what cost*? What does it cost each of us to hold back? Part of you may feel you don't want to share and that's okay. Perhaps you feel you can't share what happened (confidential grief), and this oftentimes comes from the stigma in our professional community around client suicide. This was again evident when I outreached several colleagues for interviews surrounding this book. One of the first questions from several of them indicated a worry that I would "out" them to the community, with fear of criticism and judgment being the result.

My Colleagues Will Judge Me.

Let's be honest, we make snap judgments of one another as humans, so why would colleagues be different? Oftentimes our assumptions of colleagues' responses or views of us are more harsh or black and white than what is actually true. However, there's something to sit with in how intense our judgment or reaction is to a colleague whose client dies by suicide. Do we have a snap judgment of their professionalism? Do we feel triggered by their story? It's important to normalize the impact a client suicide has on the professional experiencing it, as well as their network when it's public knowledge. Until we change our thinking on a larger scale about client suicide and professional responsibility, our colleagues who are part of the 25% will continue to hold this experience in private. More ideas on community response that are helpful instead of harmful are included in Chapter 12.

My Supervisor Will Fire Me.

Having to speak with other professionals one-on-one is another relational worry that is articulated frequently after a client suicide. Since you are already battling with your own questions about responsibility, it's natural to extend that worry to your supervisor(s). Is it possible we will be released from supervision because of a client suicide? Will they fire us? I truly hope not, but it is a possibility if negligence is found on behalf of the therapist. How can supervisors support their supervisees who've experienced a client suicide? Check out some tips in Chapter 13.

My Community Won't Trust Me.

Extending beyond our colleagues and our practice, our community can have their own response to learning that we've lost a client to suicide, especially because they don't get the details or the full picture as we continue to honor client confidentiality. Do they have their own judgments? Is there fear? Is there a community member asking a ton of questions with the hope that it will help them prevent a suicide in their own life? How can we support professionals who are grieving the loss of a client suicide as part of a community? More thoughts are found in Chapter 12.

I'll Be Reported to My Licensing Board.

Of all the relational fears, this one feels significantly loaded. What if, as the clinician experiencing the loss of a client to suicide, we are reported to our licensing board by a colleague or community member? What if they don't have the full story but file a complaint anyway? This action step feels like a cruel punishment when put in motion by someone who isn't fully in the know. Oftentimes, it also speaks to their own fears for them to pursue a grievance with minimal information. If you do decide to disclose details of your client's death to a trusted colleague or supervisor and a grievance is filed by that person in response to your honest disclosure, it can feel like a significant relationship rupture when you admit fault or identify steps you should have taken but didn't. It's a slippery slope of vulnerability to share what happened, with the ethical obligation to take steps when a professional makes an egregious mistake. The hope is that this isn't happening often due to clinicians not being at fault in any way for their clients' deaths, yet the fear of someone finding fault and taking this painful step keeps many therapists up at night.

Mental

- I'm incompetent.
- I can't be trusted to keep others safe.
- I didn't do enough.
- I'll lose my license.
- I should leave the field.
- I should stop using that modality.
- I need more training.
- I can't do this.
- What if this happens again?

- Who will be next?
- What was I missing?
- What can I ask other clients to feel reassured that they are safe?
- How can I prevent this from happening again?

I'm Incompetent.

Speaking of things that keep professionals up at night, an array of negative or anxious thoughts is common when your client dies by suicide. At the top of the list lands anxiety about competency within this profession. It sounds like, "I don't know what I'm doing. I'm bad at this. I'm a bad therapist." It's part of the self-blame experience where we feel pressure to be perfect, be professional, and keep all our clients alive.

I Can't Be Trusted to Keep Others Safe.

Amid the grief, the thought of being untrustworthy follows close on the heels of feelings of incompetency. Other ways it can sound include, "If I couldn't help them, how can I help anyone else? If I couldn't keep them alive, how do I keep my other clients alive?" This self-doubt is damaging both personally and professionally.

I Didn't Do Enough.

How do you know if you did enough? If you wrack your brain for all the details before your client's death, do you find some aspect that you could have changed? Even if you fought to get them a higher level of care or hospitalized them to keep them safe, did it really just lengthen their life without taking away the risk of suicide? It's hard to know what, if anything, would have made a difference after the fact. After all, people still maintain their autonomy to choose to live or die.

I'll Lose My License.

Naturally, in feeling a lack of competence and trust in your abilities on the heels of a client suicide, you may go from the fear of losing your license to the belief that it's inevitable. With this belief comes different behaviors. Do we go through the motions with clients? Do we start canceling appointments? Do we prepare to transfer clients and quit? A licensing board review can be a lengthy process, adding to the personal torture and trauma state experienced when losing a client to suicide.

I Should Leave the Field.

Quitting or exiting the field may be one piece that brings us some mental comfort in this difficult time after our client's suicide. Not because the idea itself is pleasant, but because it gives us a sense of control regarding our future. This may be especially true as you go through a formal review with a licensing board, another painful process alongside your client's death. Compounded by current grief and loss symptoms and an overall disruption in personal and professional functioning, quitting may feel easier than trying to heal amid the ongoing demands of our profession.

I Should Stop Using That Modality.

If quitting isn't the loudest option ringing through our minds, we may conclude that we need to stop the modality we were using with the client who died. Paired with the outcome of their death, we may falsely believe that the modality in progress was part of the problem, or that we are not skilled enough to keep using it. Similar to food poisoning leading to an active avoidance of the food paired with extreme discomfort and illness, our modality may end up being the aspect we reject or avoid in the hopes of not having another client die by suicide while in our care.

I Need More Training.

As we consciously reject modalities associated with our client's death, we may conclude that we need more training or new trainings to help ourselves and our other clients. This can understandably show up as pursuing additional training in suicide assessment or safety planning, especially if our initial training was limited, which is often the case of most mental health professionals. This can also show up as investing in a new modality that feels more in alignment with the work we want to do going forward.

I Can't Do This.

Sometimes tied into the decision to embrace new modalities is the decision to "not work with suicidal clients." As you can imagine, not working with suicidal clients is hard to believe since suicide is a human experience, not limited to psychopathology. In other words, even the healthiest of people can have a suicidal thought, so to say we don't work with suicide is inaccurate. Taking the stance that we don't work with suicide may actually mean that we refuse to ask the question about suicide, which comes with its own list of problems and risks. Not bringing it up in the therapy space doesn't make it go away. Additionally, the thought "I can't do this" can show up as a blanket belief about our overall functioning, heard loudly on repeat within our minds as we attempt to cope with significant stress from the suicide loss.

What if This Happens Again?

Struggling to handle the intensity of our grief after a client's death means that we can also have the thought of it happening again. If you feel that you are barely keeping it together with the current tragedy, the possibility of another client loss to suicide can feel overwhelming and alarming. It can evolve into persistent feelings of helplessness and fear, or, at the other end of the spectrum, a level of jadedness where another suicide feels inevitable.

Who Will Be Next?

In response to anxiety and fear of another client suicide, you may find your mind is trying to anticipate the next loss, such as attempting to predict who on your caseload is most at risk or next in line for suicide. Paired with hypervigilance and rumination, this can make a clinician sick with worry, and can alter their behaviors toward a focus exclusively on risk management rather than authentic therapeutic connection.

What Was I Missing?

An ongoing thought amid rumination and thought spirals is the question of what was missed for the client who died. Do we come to the conclusion that we missed something? Do we determine that there was actually nothing else we could do? Or do we land somewhere in between? These mental gymnastics can haunt us for months after our client's death, changing how we interact with other clients in the therapeutic space.

What Can I Ask Other Clients to Feel Reassured That They Are Safe?

In an effort not to miss something with other clients, we may be seeking out the magic question to better assess a client's risk for suicide. Is it asking about suicide more often? Differently? With scaling questions? Is it safety planning or gathering multiple formal suicide assessments to use with your current caseload? The knee-jerk behavioral response is to dial up how often we ask about suicide, which lands well at an intake or with acutely suicidal clients, but can be hit or miss for folks with chronic suicidality where suicide is a common participant in their everyday experience with minimal risks at present.

How Can I Prevent This from Happening Again?

The big question for most professionals is how to prevent suicide from happening again. Can you prevent suicide through a caring conversation with your clients? Can you lean into their suicide story? Suicide prevention is possible when clients want to talk about it and have hope that something will shift for the better. Suicide is about pain, and talking about their pain with someone who wants to help can be empowering for folks. According to the U.S. Department of Health and Human Services (2023), there are warning signs for suicide, which helps us as clinicians to feel like there's something we can do. Pursuing additional training in suicide assessment and prevention can be one step toward feeling more prepared, although it doesn't prevent suicide from ever happening again. There is a small subset of people that we can't help because they are determined to die, and then die by suicide without saying anything to anyone. So knowing this, how do we continue forward, adapting and engaging in meaningful work we offer clients through therapy?

Spiritual

- Did I encourage this?
- Did I somehow collude on their wish to die?
- Is everyone suicidal?
- What if I'm suicidal?
- What if I become suicidal?
- What if it makes sense why they chose to die?
- Do I support Death with Dignity?
- Would this feel different if it had been a terminal illness?
- What happens after we die?

Did I Encourage This?

Exploring adaptation from a spiritual place, a part of our work after a client death by suicide is sitting in our own beliefs and values about life and death. What are your beliefs about dying? How about dying with dignity? Would your grief experience around your client's death look different if your client died from a terminal illness? Are you able to explore your client's quality of life from a place of curiosity, where factors for suicide feel more probable? What are your thoughts on client autonomy and how you support autonomy in therapy? It's oftentimes challenging to equally hold for a client's authentic suicide experience while wanting to help them, although it is possible.

Did I Somehow Collude on Their Wish to Die?

Pam Rycroft's words can land like a punch to the gut. "In not finding the right words to dissuade her from her view, was I in fact colluding with the idea of death as the only solution?" (Weiner, 2005). As a professional attempting to balance a client's right to live or die with the desire to keep folks alive, how is this communicated? How do we sit in the discomfort of their disclosures that death may be "easier"? If we can see their quality of life declining, does this influence our ability to hold space for their desires to live versus their desires to die? How do we honor their views without agreeing that death is an option? I hear my own voice in my head from training hundreds of clinicians on suicide assessment over the years where I say, "don't make the mistake of telling a client what their protective factors are; let them tell you." Assuming something or someone is keeping your client alive isn't helpful, nor is convincing them to stay alive through a verbal contract. As your client's therapist, you will need to find that delicate balance between honoring their disclosures and thoughts about death without saying yes to suicide.

Is Everyone Suicidal?

When a client dies by suicide, it can bring suicide to the front of your mind where it feels ever-present, kind of like when you buy a new car and you see that same car everywhere on the road. Or like when you have decided to get pregnant and see pregnant women everywhere you go. With over 12 million people (American Association of Suicidology 2023) having had a suicidal thought, it's not exactly wrong to wonder if everyone is suicidal, especially because it's part of being human. The task at hand is not to embrace a jaded viewpoint where we place everyone into the same box, resulting in thoughts and behaviors that pathologize people rather than leaning into their unique stories of life, death, and suicide.

What if I'm Suicidal?

As humans, clinicians can also have their own suicidal thoughts. What if helping clients navigate their suicidal thoughts exacerbates our own? Not that talking about their suicidal thoughts gives us the idea of suicide—we already know that is a myth. Rather, talking about suicide brings our own thoughts of suicide more to the surface, front and center in a way that we can't ignore. It goes without saying that we would want to seek our own support to navigate this experience, whether it be explored in supervision as part of countertransference, or in our own personal therapy to support our health and wellness goals. Additionally, what if a client's death by suicide contributes to a personalized suicide contagion effect, where our own desires to die are amplified as part of this loss? Do we feel a sense of hopelessness in losing our client to suicide, worrying that our own suicidal thoughts made us normalize things too much or caused us to miss something? Are we drowning in shame or responsibility because we feel we weren't "healthy enough" to help our client effectively? This too is something to seek supervision or consultation around because of how grief puts blinders on our understanding of events. Just like with our clients, we don't have to navigate these worries or our own suicidal thoughts alone.

What if I Become Suicidal?

In response to significant grief and loss, depression and suicidal thoughts of your own may develop, especially if you have a dark, ugly narrative in your head that's playing loudly on repeat. Suicidal thoughts are even more possible if you aren't sleeping. If you are finding yourself at fault. If you are worried about losing everything as the result of a licensing board investigation. What if things were already a little rocky in your life before your client's death, and this feels like the last straw? Or what if you have had suicidal thoughts of your own previously and worry they will return? Several of the therapists I interviewed shared a deeper compassion for clients with chronic suicidality in having worked with their own suicidal thoughts. Their lived experience of the pain made them show up even more for their clients, allowing them to lean in instead of pulling back.

What if It Makes Sense Why They Chose to Die?

This question is coming up more and more within the professional community because of terminal illnesses and quality-of-life questions. Especially as we track a population of older folks 75+ who are choosing to die by suicide (American Association of Suicidology 2023) rather than experience a slow, painful decline in functioning followed by death. As humans, we are built to avoid pain. What if there is physical pain or functional decline that is contributing to suicide being an option for a client? Human to human, we can understand why suicide is showing up as an option. If we put ourselves in their shoes, we may even have a similar thought. Depending on your own work, this thought can be comforting, neutral, or alarming. I invite you to notice what shows up for you and do some work with what you discover.

Do I Support Death with Dignity?

First defined as medically assisted suicide for people with terminal illnesses in the state of Oregon, the movement toward more states allowing Death with Dignity provides another area of self-reflection. Knowing that this involves a lengthy process of multiple psychological interviews and tasks for a client to complete, how does this land for you as a professional when it relates to suicide and client suicide?

Would This Feel Different if It Had Been a Terminal Illness?

One just has to read *Me Before You* (2012) by author Jojo Moyes to sit in the mix of emotions that show up as the main character pursues purposeful death before his terminal illness chooses his death date for him. His quality of life appears to improve when he meets a new love interest, but—spoiler alert—nothing she can say or do will change his mind about his death timeline. For many readers, this brings up the turmoil we experience within ourselves in seeing multiple sides to his decision. Understanding his wish to die with dignity. Recognizing the "what-ifs" for the years he could have left, which could be meaningful and full of love and purpose. Honoring how he doesn't want to invite his new love into a painful decline where she watches him wither and suffer before her eyes. There's a lot to unpack around how we, as professionals and as people, conceptualize death from terminal illness and death from suicide.

What Happens After We Die?

Coming full circle, a final spiritual component to explore is our beliefs about what happens after death. This may be amplified by your client's death by suicide and your desire for conscious closure and healing after the fact. Do your beliefs bring you comfort? Do they make your grief work more intense? Do you feel at peace knowing they are no longer suffering? Or are you haunted by their choice and the outcome for their spiritual self? As professionals, we work with people of diverse backgrounds who require compassion and neutrality, regardless of whether their views and spiritual beliefs are similar to ours or not. Therefore it's important to recognize our own beliefs about life and death and do our own work around them, in order to show up thoughtfully and to prevent unintentional harm to the suicidal clients we serve.

Hopefully this in-depth look at PERMS (Castro Croy 2022) doesn't exactly surprise you, since the ideas and experiences listed are similar to Post-Traumatic Stress Disorder (PTSD) symptoms and echo the experience of a medical professional losing a patient, which serves as another impactful grief experience for professional helpers. It's also important to name that you don't necessarily have to endorse all these symptoms to recognize the lasting effect of a client suicide on your functioning as a clinician. For the therapists I interviewed for this book, a common thread was the shift from acute symptoms immediately after learning of their client's death by suicide, to stabilization and a reduction of symptoms several months or years later through processing and adapting after the loss. Let's get to know several of these therapists and their stories in the next chapter.

Introducing Therapist Stories of Client Suicide

10

ANOTHER WAY TO VIEW a clinician's response to client suicide is on a spectrum. Picture hypervigilance and anxiety on one end of the spectrum with jadedness and depression on the other as polar opposites and extremes. In finding themselves therapist survivors, colleagues may notice that they are jumping out of their skin in anticipation of "doing better" and "seeing the signs" next time in their clinical work, in contrast to colleagues who may feel jaded toward the potential of future client loss. This jadedness is more possible when experiencing multiple client suicides, coupled with feelings of helplessness, depression, and burnout. Outwardly, one is trying their hardest to prevent a suicide from happening again, whereas the other may feel it's inevitable.

Annabelle

Annabelle enjoyed working in her private practice with driven professionals who were experiencing anxiety and depression. She was skilled in Cognitive Behavioral Therapy (CBT) and made it a priority to coordinate her clients' care with their medical professionals, especially when it came to medication changes. Annabelle was devastated to receive a voicemail from her client's partner that he had died by suicide the weekend between their scheduled appointments. He had expressed life dissatisfaction and mild depression symptoms for months, but had not indicated that he would act on his fleeting suicidal thoughts. Her client had denied plans, means, or intent when asked by Annabelle in multiple sessions in their therapeutic work for the past eight months.

Annabelle's initial response to learning of her client's suicide was that of intense fear. She was worried she had missed something that could have saved his life, leaving her crushed by the weight of responsibility. She felt immense shame and began to question her ability to help other clients due to feeling blindsided by this client's death. After taking a day off to compose herself, Annabelle resumed working with her clients, oftentimes feeling half present as she wracked her brain for the missing piece of her client's story. Annabelle chose to suppress her grief, only grieving in private for fear of being judged by her peers as an incompetent clinician.

Four months after her client's death, Annabelle confided in a colleague. Initially she had been holding her breath to see if the partner was going to hold Annabelle responsible for her client's death. When she felt ready to talk, Annabelle chose a colleague who worked in suicide prevention, hoping they would be gentler with her. Annabelle had lost a significant amount of weight in four months and her autoimmune condition had flared up, leaving her pale, puffy, and fatigued. She was preparing to spend some time with her family to regroup and had reduced her caseload to make things feel more manageable.

Jeremy

Jeremy was a counselor working in a substance treatment center that focused on co-occurring disorders. He was six months into his current job when his client died by suicide. Jeremy had been tracking some additional stressors with his client as part of his relapse prevention plan, only to learn that his client died after his spouse asked for a divorce. Jeremy was left reeling, reflecting on how steady his client had been in seeking therapy to better himself and how it hadn't been enough to keep him alive.

After the initial shock, Jeremy's response to his client's death encompassed anger, sadness, and hypervigilance to keep other clients safe. He found himself compulsively asking all of his clients about suicide multiple weeks in a row. He sought out suicide assessment trainings and began collecting assessments he could administer with clients in the hopes of keeping them alive.

Jeremy's response to his client's suicide impacted him personally and relationally as well. He was more irritable, defensive, and on edge. He perceived any feedback from his spouse or his director at work as criticism and questioned his worth to his friends and family. Jeremy had his own substance history that was being challenged by this event, with cravings to use again to numb himself from the experience of his client's suicide.

Lorel

Lorel was enjoying working for herself in private practice. She was aware of client suicides happening to her colleagues in her previous employment in a hospital setting, and felt fortunate that she hadn't had that experience herself. Lorel was working with a client with chronic suicidality who was well resourced and committed to coming to weekly therapy to better herself. So Lorel felt understandably alarmed when her client missed her scheduled appointment and her phone was turned off when Lorel attempted to call. Listening to her gut, Lorel called her client's emergency contact, who proceeded to call Lorel back after finding her client dead by suicide.

Out of a desire to help, Lorel didn't initially allow herself to feel the immense grief of the loss of her client. Instead, she attempted to help the emergency contact who'd found her client with their own loss. This meant holding space for the person to share and grieve in the hours that followed, only fully experiencing her own symptoms of grief after Lorel finished the call.

Lorel's grief showed up primarily in her body. She experienced months of tearfulness, sleep disruption, tension headaches, and loss of appetite. She was hit by waves of sadness and fatigue. She knew she wouldn't hear from family because her client had none. Yet Lorel felt that there was some other piece that was absent, a piece she needed to fully heal from her client's suicide. Something was missing.

Evie

Evie was passionate about working with teens and adults. She'd built a group practice to serve these populations and loved helping her team enhance their skills. It felt like the wind was knocked out of her when she got the call from a parent that her teen client (pronouns they/them) had died by suicide. Her client had been wicked smart and a star athlete, yet they'd been struggling for a few months now and had a safety plan in place with their parents due to increased suicidal thoughts. Their psychiatry appointment to revisit medication was scheduled for the following week. But it hadn't been fast enough.

Evie felt that she'd failed her client and their parents and now the tragedy would impact Evie, her team, and the larger community that loved her client as a star athlete on a well-known sports team. Evie had received the heartbreaking call and then saw the posts in a social media group connected to her teen client's school hours later. She felt the loss all over again as she saw people responding to the news, expressing their own pain and posting memories of her client online.

The loss of this young person was becoming more and more real for Evie as the hours passed. Evie noticed how she was having flashbacks to how they had looked in their last session. Seeing in her mind's eye where they'd sat on the couch. Replaying their words, recalling their body language, trying to look for some hidden message of their plans to die. It didn't help that she saw her client's face on the news throughout the week as a local channel picked up the story.

Alejandra

Alejandra was a spiritual person and a therapist known for her warmth, her inclusivity, and her grounded, supportive approach with suicidal clients in her private practice. Alejandra was transparent with her clients about her own history of suicidal thoughts and had abundant compassion for talking with clients about their own. It was several years into her practice that her client stopped coming to sessions abruptly. Although her client had chronic suicidality, Alejandra did not see any blatant signs of her being at imminent risk of danger to herself, so she completed her usual outreach in an attempt to reengage her client. There was no response to her efforts to reengage, and Alejandra assumed her client had ghosted her, as was a popular practice with therapy at the time.

It was several months later that Alejandra got the email from her client's parent, stating they had accessed her client's account and saw the outreach attempts from Alejandra, and had decided to email Alejandra to notify her that her client had died by suicide months earlier. Alejandra was stunned and sad at this news. In the email, the parent emphasized that Alejandra had been mentioned by her client to family members, and had stated how much their work together had helped her. Although Alejandra was relieved to be given this gift of reassurance from her client's parents, she was also experiencing a heaviness in her body in response to her client's death by suicide.

Alejandra's response to her client's death by suicide incorporated her own spiritual practice into her grief work. Although Alejandra honored the urge to revisit her notes from their last few sessions together, it came more from a place of wanting to recall where things left off than a desire to protect herself. Upon seeing that her notes indicated no cause for worry, Alejandra began processing the heaviness in her body tied to her client's death.

Steps for Healing From Client Suicide **11**

I S THERE A HAPPY MEDIUM between having sole responsibility for keeping a client alive and supporting client autonomy and choice as a therapist? I like to think so. Even when we are successful at focusing on our client instead of ourselves, we are still significantly impacted by our client's suicide. So what can we do to support our own healing? How do we help the 25% of us who will have a client die by suicide? I introduce the possibility of healing from suicide as the concept of lean on, lean in. Let's take a look at LEAN.

> L: Listen to your needs
> E: Embrace grief and loss work
> A: Ask for help
> N: Name meaning

Listen to Your Needs

When you first get the news of your client's death, what do you need in that moment? Do you need a safe space to have a good cry? Would you like to cancel your clients and go home? Do you need to talk to your supervisor or a trusted colleague? Would you prefer to stay grounded by continuing to work through the end of the workday? Each clinician's needs are going to look different, and we should attempt to remain curious about those needs in any given moment.

Your needs may vary based on a couple of factors—factors like (1) how long you'd worked with your client, (2) what kind of therapeutic relationship you had, and (3) how the news was delivered to you. The duration of your client work has an impact, meaning the severity of your grief and loss response may depend on the length and quality of the relationship. For example, a client you met once for an intake will still have an impact on you when you learn of their death by suicide, but it may have a very different impact compared to a client you've seen weekly for two years. Your role also matters. If you are their individual therapist, we can assume a closer, more connected relationship than if you were a group therapy co-facilitator, where the client was a participant you only interacted with through group work parameters.

The method of delivery for this traumatic news also matters. When interviewing colleagues for this book, I noticed a relationship between their immediate response and symptoms, with the news being delivered by staff, phone call, voicemail, email, or text. As you can imagine, the clinicians who have news delivered over the phone by a loved one may receive more information than a text or voicemail could provide. The person on the other end of the phone may share details of how their client was found, what they looked like, or the person may illuminate the circumstances leading up to their client's death. It's both a blessing and a curse for those of us who've experienced a client suicide in this way, because we get answers to some of our questions while also risking the introduction of haunting and disturbing imagery. Additionally, we may drop into professional mode in order to help the distressed caller delivering this news (like Lorel), which delays our own natural grief response.

In contrast, the news of our client's suicide by text, voicemail, or email can feel cold or detached. Some clinicians prefer it this way to allow them the privacy of grieving in real time without anyone there to witness it. Grief can be messy, and oftentimes we don't want the other person to witness ours as they deal with their own. However, some therapists are left wanting answers, with the urge to connect with the person who delivered this heavy news to know more.

Jeremy

Jeremy craved logic in feeling baffled by his client's death. He wanted to know what had happened, which showed up as a strong urge to call the spouse of his client to learn more. Was he allowed to call them? He wasn't sure. Although Jeremy had felt at odds with the treatment center director at times, he felt comfortable with his direct supervisor. Therefore Jeremy sought out his supervisor first to see if this was permitted within their treatment center policies. I hear it often as a mental health leader, supervisors and legal professionals will deter us from speaking to a client's loved ones after their suicide from a place of caution and CYA, which can prevent conscious closure for us as professionals. Fortunately, Jeremy's supervisor engaged him with curiosity to further unpack his motives for calling his client's spouse, while also exploring Jeremy's own needs after this loss.

Embrace Grief and Loss Work

This may feel like a given, and yet so many professionals attempt to "push through" and keep going rather than slowing down to do their own grief and loss work. They may continue to work, avoid thinking about their client, compartmentalize (which has its place in the short term) or self-medicate in any of the ways our clients do when a traumatic event happens. So how do we embrace our own grief and loss work?

- Movement
- Processing
- Conscious closure

Movement

Since trauma is all about activation, meaning our sympathetic nervous system response, movement can help. Is it about pacing as you take in information? Are you walking to allow yourself some time and space without feeling emotionally flooded? Does movement serve as a cathartic release for your grief? By no means is sitting still the only option for deep reflection in your grief work. In fact, many of the driven professionals, perfectionists, and therapists I serve find the idea of sitting still repulsive and uncomfortable. So why not try movement? It can't hurt when we think of the positives of movement for thinking, blood circulation, and breathing, all of which can help address the physical and mental symptoms we can experience after a client's death by suicide.

Processing

What helps you take in and process the event of your client's suicide? Is it talking to someone? Is it hearing your voice say things aloud? Is it journaling, writing, or an audio file to remember what this was like for you? Is it talking to your client as if they were here? Joining a support group for other therapists to not feel alone? Reading a book on suicide and healing from suicide? I offer this book as one of the many tools at your disposal for processing. More tools for your grief work after a client suicide can be found in Chapter 14.

Conscious Closure

I first heard this phrase from a seasoned client who was describing her goodbye with her previous therapist. They had been working together for several years, and my client was having a hard time with the idea of things ending. Conscious describes awareness, as in being fully aware and present in that experience. Therefore conscious closure can be defined as being present in the ending of a relationship. To be intentional with how it ends. To see meaning and invite reflection on the relationship itself. How could this not apply to the end of a relationship with your client who has died by suicide?

Evie

Evie knew she needed some support after her client's death. As a group practice owner, she felt some pressure to be strong, put-together, and present for her team in their grief response, making it hard for her to do her own work. She sought out an online support group for therapists who had a client die by suicide, carving out space weekly to reflect and process her grief in the safety of a group of colleagues who held zero judgment and made no demands of her. In finding the group immensely helpful, Evie knew she wanted to give back to her local community by starting an in-person support group for therapists someday.

Ask for Help

Healing from client suicide is not something we do alone. We are social creatures, so connecting with others, even when in immense pain, can have a healing effect. One study by Hammond (1991) found that having a supportive community reduced the risk of developing Post-Traumatic Stress Disorder (PTSD; Weiner 2005). Since helping professionals are also known to develop these symptoms in response to a client death by suicide (Weiner 2005), community matters. Who do you feel you can ask for help? Is it your supervisor or boss? What if you work for yourself in private practice? Do you have a few trusted colleagues who could hold this for you and help you feel safe? Do you want to reach out to colleagues who've also experienced a client suicide? Resisting the urge to ask for help looks like self-sabotage on your journey to healing from client suicide. It doesn't serve you to suffer in silence and can have a lasting effect on your mind, body, and spirit, much like what we've heard so far for Annabelle. So think about it now if a client suicide hasn't happened to you. Who would be on your list of colleagues to reach out to? Much like carving out time and a plan for your professional will, carving out a plan for the tragedy of a client suicide can feel heavy but also helpful.

Lorel

Lorel was at a loss for who to speak to about her client's death. She continued to feel the waves of emotion in sudden tearfulness and a persistent loss of appetite. Lorel wanted to move toward healing. She decided to reach out to a colleague she'd heard speak at a local conference several years before. They were someone who had shared their own vulnerable story of client suicide with a mass audience, and had shown up as authentic and compassionate on stage. Lorel began working with them as a consultant and support person for her own story of client suicide, revisiting the ever-present feeling that something was missing from her healing journey that would grant her more closure after her client's death.

Name Meaning

With time, the hope is to find meaning in your client's death by suicide. There is no set time for this to come to some sort of resolution, just as there is no timeline for grief. Let me be clear, discovering meaning doesn't indicate you are okay with their death, although you may find yourself closer to acceptance that it happened. With this acceptance comes an invitation to make meaning from this life-altering experience. Do you discover personal meaning connected to your values and perspectives of life and death? Do you look at the experience of suicide through new eyes? Do you uncover deep compassion for yourself and colleagues going through this experience? Do you feel spurred to speak on this topic or train others on suicide? Do you feel compelled to write a book? Whether your meaning is found specific to your client, yourself, or to the experience of suicide at large, there can be something incredibly powerful in naming your meaning aloud. Who can you share it with? Who can witness the transformation it spurs within you?

Alejandra

Alejandra dug down deep into her spiritual beliefs after her client's death by suicide. She had freed herself of the possible burden of responsibility, which left her more able to reflect on her client's experience and the meaning in their actions to die. Alejandra revisited her own history of suicidal thoughts, as well as parts work, to determine that her client had made a decision she thought was best for herself. Alejandra felt it to her core that it wasn't her responsibility to keep clients alive; rather, it was her responsibility to create a safe space for them to talk about suicide.

To lean on others is hard. To lean in can feel even harder. Jeremy, Evie, Lorel, and Alejandra had their own ways of moving toward healing, and at their own pace. What about Annabelle? She had been paralyzed by fear connected to her client's suicide, and it had prevented her from leaning in to the work, nor was she leaning on others. True, she'd shared her client's death with one colleague months later. Yes, she determined she needed some time off. But it was only after several months of her mind, body, and spirit declining that she'd made these decisions. How do we help Annabelle and other clinicians not suffer in silence, at the detriment of their own health? It boils down to the helpful and hurtful things we say and do as a community of professionals who have a client die by suicide.

Community Response to Client Suicide

12

I T MAY NOT SURPRISE YOU to know that crafting this list of the hurtful responses someone can say to our client's suicide was easy. Almost too easy. One colleague I spoke with reflected that people put therapists on a pedestal. We are supposed to embody what our clients aspire to be and must continue to function at that level. Us being human isn't embraced as readily from this high standard, reinforcing a problematic belief that we can't be both experts and human. Additionally, suicide stirs up emotions and fears in others that can come out of their mouths as projections onto us. It speaks to their hope that if they interrogate us and ask us all the "right" questions, a client suicide won't happen to them. I wish this piece were true, that asking all the questions of a colleague about their client suicide prevented other client suicides, but as we've already established, suicide is complicated. Let's take a look at some hurtful responses experienced by professionals who've had a client die by suicide followed by more helpful ones.

Hurtful Community Responses

- Couldn't you see it coming?
- What happened?!
- Your client committed suicide?
- They were selfish.
- You couldn't see it coming.

Couldn't You See It Coming?

This question comes directly and indirectly from our communities in how they ask the question. It's right up there with "couldn't you see the signs?" Or the more aggressive and implied "you must have missed something because now they're dead." Our communities believe that we, as professionals, should know more than the average person based on our training and skills, which translates to our ability to keep our clients alive. It feeds a grossly misunderstood belief that it's our *job* to keep people alive. Is it though? Allow yourself to remain curious about the ongoing debate of our job being to help people versus keeping them alive.

What Happened?!

Although this question can be delivered with empathy, it still has an undercurrent of responsibility and fault. "What did you miss?" Does this question imply we weren't paying attention? Negligence? Incompetence? This question feels loaded because it is.

Your Client Committed Suicide?

Per the introduction of this book, you know that suicide prevention entities are working hard to remove the word *committed* from our language of suicide. *Committed* implies they did something wrong. Committed as in committed a crime. It's an uphill battle to remove this word from all sources. Asking this as a question versus stating it as a fact still stings for the professional whose client has died by suicide.

They Were Selfish.

Not so much a question as a statement, this is not anything close to helpful. Even if your personal belief is that your client was selfish, it's not something we want communities to believe. How are the client's loved ones supposed to feel when hearing this? How are you supposed to feel when hearing it? Although the person saying this statement may be trying to absolve you of responsibility, it doesn't land right. The sooner we can have people remove this sentence from their response to folks experiencing suicide personally or professionally, the better.

You Couldn't See It Coming.

Does this one feel like déjà vu? We started this list with the accusatory question of "couldn't you see it coming?" That first question implied responsibility. This second statement implies a lack of responsibility. It's not helpful either. One of my interviewees shared that folks would say this to them with the intention of it being comforting without knowing the full story. How do they know we couldn't see it coming? What if we were in fact at fault in some way? Their statement attempts to absolve us of guilt without leaning into our story, which oftentimes feels dismissive and serves as an opportunity to change the subject to something less painful instead.

Evie

Evie knew her community was hurting. Because they were a well-known teen athlete, people knew her client and had celebrated her client's successes for the past few years. They had no idea her client had been struggling in private. Evie's initial attempt at receiving support for her own grief did not go well. She couldn't confide in her team in being their leader. She didn't have an active supervisor in being licensed and in her own practice. Her colleagues showed their limited capacity by asking what happened, but could not sit in it long enough for Evie to feel fully supported. Thankfully, she had found the online support group that could wade as deeply into the pain with her as she wanted to go, giving her permission to feel the full range of emotions she had been holding onto and needing to say aloud to begin to heal.

By no means is this an exhaustive list of the uncomfortable or potentially harmful things people can say in response to our client's suicide. Their actions can speak as loud as their words. Is their response one of avoidance? Fear? Interrogation? Are they squirming in their seat? Avoiding eye contact? Fidgeting? I get it, suicide is heavy. Much like death and dying, we don't like to sit in it for long. This is very apparent to clinicians who disclose a client death by suicide, when folks acknowledge the loss and move on as quickly as possible to something else. Next, let's look at some helpful community responses instead.

Helpful Community Responses

- I'm so sorry this happened to you.
- How can we support you?
- Do you want to talk about it?
- What do you need?

I'm So Sorry This Happened to You.

Although this one isn't a question, it's a powerful acknowledgment of the pain and disruption in the clinician's life. If our knee-jerk response is to avoid pain, and thus avoid talking about client suicide, this sentence, when delivered authentically and with compassion, can go a long way to helping therapists heal.

How Can We Support You?

A meaningful question, this one represents the feeling of community in knowing that people want to help. What would be your response to this question? Do you need them to listen? Their help to access resources? Or to drop off food? Your grief process to your client's death can echo other community responses to death, which may mean food and check-ins from people who are thinking of you during this difficult time.

Do You Want to Talk About It?

This question feels like gold to me. In a world that isn't sure how to respond to death by suicide, an invitation to talk openly about it feels freeing. Like we can finally take a breath. Bringing our shoulders down from around our ears. Like we can finally open the box that we shoved this tragedy into in order to function, if only for a moment. Obviously professionals can determine when they want to share and how much they want to share. It depends on the person asking and there is still the fear of judgment or being found at fault that might deter a clinician from opening up. Regardless of whether we share or not, the question feels like a gift when delivered by someone we trust.

What Do You Need?

Similar in flavor to the question of how to support us, this question comes from my trainings in couples therapy. Asking with a compassionate tone is key. What if we need a hug? A good cry? What if we need to be left alone? Or have a need to not have to think about feeding ourselves tonight? What if we need a healthy distraction? Asking what we need can give a clinician permission to state their needs in any given moment, even if those needs change from one moment to the next.

Lorel

Lorel had felt alone and adrift in grieving as a solo private practice therapist. She wasn't sure who to turn to until she remembered the colleague who spoke of their own client suicide on stage. When starting to work with that person, one of the first things they asked Lorel was how her support had looked in the days after her client's death. Lorel expressed gratitude for her spouse, who had held space for her grief without asking questions and had provided physical proximity and comfort, which had felt helpful at the time. Lorel was now longing for a deeper connection to her client's suicide, a space to talk in detail without traumatizing her spouse in the process. She shared how thankful she was for the opportunity to work with a colleague who fully understood what it was like to lose someone this way.

Our healing journey from client suicide also involves the response of colleagues, directors, and supervisors. As Weiner (2005) states, "the response of immediate colleagues and supervisors is often a mirroring of the prevailing attitude within the field of mental health." So what attitude do we want to convey? It's probably not this first list, although many colleagues have unfortunately experienced these responses, which only serve to reinforce the stigma of suicide in our field.

Hurtful Colleague Responses

- Cover your ass.
- Let's look closely at your notes.
- What did you do?
- You really messed up.
- You should have . . .
- Don't talk to the family.
- Don't go to the service.
- You must not be a good therapist.
- You've got to stay strong.
- You could stop working with suicidal clients.

Cover Your Ass.

I get it. This response is reinforced by our licensing boards, malpractice insurance companies, and lawyers. Thus it's become a natural and immediate thought for clinicians who get the news that their client has died by suicide. Why must we reinforce this belief as mental health leaders and supervisors? If we double down on this message with our thoughts and actions, are we actually implying the clinician made a mistake? Do we assume they've done something wrong? This shouldn't be the first response by our support system for therapist survivors because it adds to the traumatic aspects of a client death by suicide, including a possible relationship rupture between the clinician and their supervisor when they most need support. It can also feed the mental health spiral of self-doubt and shame for a clinician going through a client death by suicide, something we've established is immensely difficult already.

Let's Look Closely at Your Notes.
Another common response to the news of a client suicide, this request or demand by leadership also communicates fault. It feels very different to have a clinician want to review their notes for their own purposes (like Alejandra) than to have it be enforced by supervisors and directors in the hours after learning of a client's death. Since it usually occurs immediately following the tragic news, a clinician's grief response is delayed or compounded by the request to look through their notes with a fine-tooth comb. What will they find? Negligence? A missed opportunity to keep their client alive? This can feel beyond painful when the therapist is reeling from the news, feels vulnerable, and is fearful of what their leadership will find.

What Did You Do?
Although this response isn't usually this blatant, it's just below the surface of the many questions a clinician gets from supervisors and agency directors after their client's death. It's slightly camouflaged with the questions of how the client behaved in the last session. How they responded to questions of suicide. Did you ask? Did you document that you asked? Did you ask enough times and in enough ways? It's hard to imagine this series of questions not influencing a clinician to feel fearful, defensive, or unsure of their professional competence when navigating the complexities of suicide.

You Really Messed Up.
Similar to the response above, this one isn't usually said outright, but it can be implied. If a clinician answers questions from leadership about their actions with their client that feel unsatisfactory, are we not implying that they messed up? That they were responsible? That it's their fault? I think a

lot about green clinicians who may not know what to ask or how to ask it when it comes to suicide. Asking about suicide is hard, and it takes practice to deliver questions to clients confidently and with minimal anxiety. What if they *did* miss an opportunity? What if they *did* miss a sign? The hours after a client's death are probably not the time to cement these thoughts as their truth, as it eliminates the opportunity for clinicians to learn and grow. Instead, this message will most likely contribute to the clinician's feelings of incompetence and a possible exit from the field.

You Should Have . . .

When already second-guessing ourselves after a client suicide, this advice or any directives to take a particular action can hit hard. The experience either reinforces our beliefs that we did something wrong, or it lands as unhelpful when colleagues suggest solutions that don't apply to our unique client circumstance. One interviewee for this book shared an example when her client died of suicide where she received suggestions of inpatient facilities to help her client, pushing a higher level of care. Although she agreed her client would benefit from a higher level of care, her client was uninsured with no funding to make that resource a reality. Receiving suggestions or unsolicited advice of what feels like obvious solutions can feel disrespectful and judgmental when colleagues don't take the time to understand the whole picture of our suicidal client's story.

Don't Talk to the Family.

How many of us are told we can't talk to the family? We must not offer condolences or sit alongside them in their grief. Why or why not? What if the family thinks we are responsible? What if they hear our apologies about their loved one's death and think we are admitting fault? It makes me think of advice given when experiencing a fender bender with another driver on the road. The advice sounds something like, "Don't come out of your car apologizing because then you could imply it's your fault. Instead, ask if they are okay, call 911, and wait to give your statement to the officer reporting to the scene." There is this reinforced message to not talk to the other party out of the risk that they will analyze what you say or do and find blame. The same applies to family after a loved one's suicide. Or so it seems. Here are some questions for you to consider: What does this cost the clinician? What does it cost them emotionally to avoid a bereaved family member's call? To not have a conversation about the loss? To suppress their own grief response to cover their own ass? To not receive answers they might crave within a compassionate conversation with family who can fill in the gaps, serving to support the possibility of closure months or years later? The blanket response of "don't talk to the family" feels limiting and yucky from the lens of healing for both the family and the clinician grieving this loss.

Don't Go to the Service.

What's your response as a clinical supervisor? Would you encourage or discourage your clinician's participation in the funeral or memorial service of the client who has died by suicide? Do you say *no, don't go* as imagery flashes before your eyes of sending a lamb to the slaughter? That may sound dramatic, but oftentimes supervisors feel protective of their supervisees and worry that their appearance at a funeral service would put the clinician at greater risk of a lawsuit by grieving family members. What if the therapist shows their face and family targets them as responsible for their loved one's death? What if they are invited but some family members don't want them there? What do they say when a guest asks how they know the deceased? The question of attending or not attending the service is full of land mines, but it is worth processing the pros and cons in supervision in support of the clinician who is also grieving.

You Must Not Be a Good Therapist.

This one haunts therapists. They've already had the thought themselves because of their client's death and now they are receiving it from others. Oftentimes it comes from colleagues who haven't had an intimate experience with suicide. They may naively say they don't work with suicide. They may never ask about suicide. They may be fortunate enough to not yet have a client die by suicide. And with that experience comes a snap judgment that the clinician in front of them isn't a good therapist because their client died. As you can imagine, this limiting belief reduces the traumatic experience of a client dying by suicide into the black-and-white thinking of, "you're either a good therapist because your client is alive or you're a bad therapist because they died." As this book implies, there is so much more to consider in the experience of client suicide.

You've Got to Stay Strong.

What about your colleague's or supervisor's messages of "staying strong?" Although they may mean this as an encourager, it can backfire due to the implications of expecting functioning that requires pushing through our grief process. What if it's paired with a message of "there's no time for grief"? We may already have self-imposed beliefs that we should be strong. We should be able to handle things. We should contain our grief. Knowing how unhelpful this response can be to our healing, we don't need these messages reinforced by leadership if they come at the cost of swallowing our grief and at the risk of hurting us in other prolonged and painful ways.

You Could Stop Working With Suicidal Clients.

Yes and no. Since suicide is a human experience, there's no escaping it. A clinician could pivot away from higher-risk populations, a chronic suicidality specialty, co-occurring disorders, or a higher-level-of-care facility where they believe suicide is more possible. Yet for some clinicians, this message reinforces fault because they feel that they are running away and avoiding. Maybe a clinician needs a break from high-acuity cases, which their supervisor can help them with. Maybe they need to work with a different population for a while to heal and reset. For others, they want their mental health leadership to encourage them to lean into the discomfort, which might mean continuing to work with at-risk populations while seeking additional suicide assessment training and supervision. For one colleague I interviewed, they decided to become more involved in suicide prevention rather than pulling away from it.

Alejandra

Alejandra felt that she was coping relatively well with her client's death by suicide. She thought of them often, but she wasn't experiencing other lingering symptoms or distress. When her client came to mind, she felt a deep sense of compassion and sadness for them, followed by gratitude that she had known them and for the things they had taught her about the human experience of pain. Alejandra decided to share her experience with client suicide with a colleague, who in turn asked her a lot of questions. One part of their interaction didn't sit well for Alejandra after the conversation. Her colleague assumed she'd want to stop working with chronically suicidal individuals because of this client's suicide. On the contrary, Alejandra felt more motivated to lean into her clients' suicide stories having lost a client to suicide. She felt she was even more open and compassionate to their experience after this loss, and coupled with her own history of suicidal thoughts, she believed this made her an even better therapist to serve this population.

Mental health leaders, supervisors, and colleagues have a significant role in the healing journey of therapist survivors where their response in a critical moment can help or hurt the clinician who is suffering. Let's take a closer look at some helpful responses from colleagues and supervisors that positively impact a clinician who has lost a client to suicide.

Helpful Colleague Responses

- You can't control what happens outside of the therapy space.
- Some people make the decision to die.
- It's not your job to prevent death.
- What will help you heal?
- I'm here if you want to talk.
- How would you like to honor your work with your client?
- How can I support you at the anniversary?

You Can't Control What Happens Outside of the Therapy Space.

Oftentimes, you will see your clients weekly, biweekly, or monthly. In the grand scheme of things, that one hour of scheduled therapeutic time is a very small sliver of your client's life. When I train other clinicians on suicide assessment, I emphasize how we can't possibly know or control what happens outside of the therapy space. We can't know how our client is coping if they aren't sharing. We don't know if they are using adaptive or maladaptive means to handle stressors in their lives. We can't know if they are spiraling or hiding something because we aren't mind readers. Hearing this from a trusted colleague or supervisor can give a grieving clinician permission to relax into the knowing that they aren't responsible for the goings-on outside of therapy.

Some People Make the Decision to Die.

This is true, people do make the decision to die. Every single day. This statement isn't meant to absolve clinicians of any care or commitment to their client; it's meant to reinforce our understanding that clients make their own choices. Supervisors can give clinicians this perspective amid their grief, grounding them in the importance of autonomy in therapy. Just as we aren't allowed to give advice as mental health professionals, we aren't allowed to make choices for clients, including their choice to live or die.

It's Not Your Job to Prevent Death.

This may feel radical to some, but boy does it have an impact on clinicians reeling from a client death by suicide. If my job isn't to keep them alive, what is my job? Possible answer: provide a safe space to help them grow. Support them in looking at all their options in wanting to evolve. Assist in their progress toward their treatment goals. Let me be clear: this is not all-or-nothing thinking. Supervisors can emphasize that embracing a belief that it is not our job to prevent death doesn't mean we are encouraging death, nor do we support death. It doesn't mean we don't care if they live or die. It means we honor that they are the expert in own their lives and we are sticking to our role of support person. The imagery I gave clients early in my therapy career went something like this: Starting therapy with me looks like us walking side by side in the dark. We don't truly know what's coming, we can't always see what's ahead, but we're in it together. I've got a flashlight and I'm illuminating obstacles and potholes along the path, and you get to decide the direction and the pace of our adventure together. How do you describe your role to your clients?

What Will Help You Heal?

Such a powerful question to hear from leadership, it acknowledges the stress and disruption to a clinician's life while inviting self-advocacy at work. My hope is that it also conveys a willingness from colleagues, supervisors, and directors to help in ways that feel appropriate. If a clinician is indicating they are uncertain of what they need, can a colleague identify ideas they are willing to support? Can a director normalize this experience by sharing what other clinicians have benefited from as part of their healing journey? Can a supervisor disclose (if applicable) what had helped them when experiencing a client suicide? This isn't a one-and-done question, as a clinician's needs will evolve over time. It's our job as mental health leaders to start the conversation and continue to check in to support their healing journey after a client suicide.

I'm Here if You Want to Talk.

Whether this comes from a supervisor or a colleague, the gift is their willingness to hold the heaviness of a client suicide for the clinician experiencing it. Does this invitation come with compassion and zero judgment? I imagine it would need to be conveyed in this way for a therapist survivor to take them up on the offer. My best supervisor and now colleague-turned-business-partner had an open-door policy when we were both in community mental health. When her door was open, we could come in for any reason. She also referenced a "wailing wall," which meant we could come in and cry freely if needed. Her willingness to create an off ramp for big emotions kept her team regulated with their difficult client cases, and she continues to do a beautiful job of offering a judgment-free, safe zone for her current team in private practice.

How Would You Like to Honor Your Work With Your Client?

Of all the questions and offerings possible to receive from colleagues, this one speaks the loudest to me personally, most likely because this book serves to honor my client lost to suicide as well as speak to the many others who've struggled with the possibility of suicide. Notice how this question can invite a clinician to take a deep breath. Notice how it helps them soften. This gentle question does wonders for a therapist's healing journey because it implies meaningful work was done with their client, which isn't overshadowed or eliminated by their client's death by suicide. One does not exist exclusive of the other. It's not a situation of either you did good work or you didn't because they died. As mental health leaders, embracing this question serves as an invitation to reflect on the powerful work done before the tragedy. It's a gift for the clinician who's questioning their worth after a client suicide and also serves to honor the client they've lost.

How Can I Support You at the Anniversary?

This question stands out to me for lots of good reasons. One of my colleague interviewees shared how this question landed so well for her as someone who'd recently lost a client to suicide. She felt seen. She felt supported. She felt like the person delivering this question understood that our clients stay with us after death, leaving a permanent mark on our psyche. Much like other grief events, there can be a lot of support in the initial weeks or months after a client suicide, but that support dwindles as time passes. So to have a colleague ask how they could support her at the year anniversary of her client's death meant a lot. I know it would mean a lot to many therapist survivors.

Jeremy

Jeremy was days into his grief. With the help of his supervisor, he'd remained curious about the urge to call his client's spouse and had held fast, recognizing it was self-serving and not necessarily helpful to the spouse to pursue this agenda. Jeremy's supervisor checked in on him several times in that first week, offering to be someone Jeremy could talk to, or to provide colleague referrals if that felt like a better fit. What helped Jeremy the most in those first few days was hearing his supervisor say it had happened to him, too. His supervisor had also lost a client to suicide and was comfortable telling Jeremy about it. Jeremy felt more reassured and less alone in learning his supervisor—a person he respected and trusted—had also had a client die. Jeremy's supervisor was able to normalize the increased risks of suicide for the population they served, a population that was struggling with both mental health and addiction.

Supportive Leadership After Client Suicide

13

S UPERVISORS HAVE THE MOST IMPORTANT job when it comes to shaping and supporting therapists in the field. Supervisors not only serve as gatekeepers for the profession but also usually are designated as the point person to help a clinician navigate client suicide. If they aren't helping a clinician navigate a client suicide in this moment, perhaps they can prepare a clinician for this worst-case, devastating scenario. As Jason S. Spiegelman and James L. Werth Jr. stated in *Therapeutic and Legal Issues for Therapists Who Have Survived a Client Suicide* (Weiner 2005), "It is not sufficient to teach a therapist-in-training to perform a skeletal suicide assessment without preparing her or him for the possibility that the client will attempt, or worse yet die by, suicide."

Given the challenges we named in the last chapter with community, colleague, and supervisor responses to suicide, I think some ideas that embody an empowered, compassionate response by mental health leaders deserves its own chapter. Why? Because when clinicians are questioning their competence and spiraling out from grief and fear after a client death by suicide, it's our job as leaders to anchor them and help them navigate the stressful next steps so they can start their healing journey—even when we may not have the lived experience of a client suicide ourselves. We can help therapists experience post-traumatic growth, defined as positive psychological change from the aftermath of trauma, including resilience and growth from significantly challenging life events (Kaufman 2020). Client suicide is one of these events. Below are some guidelines for mental health leaders to help therapists move toward post-traumatic growth after a client suicide.

1. Help therapists heal
2. Provide regular supervisor support
3. Review case file or notes if desired
4. Help therapists see their competencies
5. Share similar experiences
6. Explore their schedule
7. Identify evolution in their client work
8. Recognize the tragedy and the positive changes that occurred afterward

Help Therapists Heal

This is a broad category because each therapist will need something different on their healing journey from client suicide. Yet it's number one on the list because this should be the first priority. Not a cover-your-ass reaction like reading through all their progress notes, not a white-knuckle-stay-strong response to their grief, but a how-can-I-help-you approach. As supervisors and leaders, we can do better at this. We can ask what our clinicians need, we can offer ideas of what has helped others, and we can be a steady presence through the turmoil they will go through for the next six to twelve months. By no means am I saying step in and be their therapist. Instead, help them find a therapist if they need one. Help them find resources and suggest books if those would help. Don't be MIA because this is hard to deal with; be present, be supportive, be a leader. Your thoughtful involvement can help amazing clinicians adapt and remain in the field when suicide loss and grief are trying to push them out.

Jeremy

Jeremy was three months into his grief and loss response to his client's suicide when his supervisor asked him about continued education. Jeremy was confused and slightly panicked, having to admit he hadn't been pursuing any new trainings or content in just trying to function and show up well for his clients each day. His supervisor reassured Jeremy that he was doing well with the clients they staffed each week in supervision, and that the focus on his own health and wellness was a priority. He shared that the treatment center had funds allocated for continued education, and Jeremy's supervisor suggested Jeremy use some of these funds for a self-care retreat for therapists that was happening next month in a warmer climate. His supervisor emphasized how it was important to step away from client care once in a while as part of burnout prevention, and suggested that Jeremy take his spouse along for a mini-vacation while Jeremy attended the presentations scheduled during the day. Jeremy was surprised and grateful for the opportunity to step away from direct client care for one week while learning something new. He said yes to the self-care retreat and was looking forward to reconnecting with his spouse after the difficult few months they'd already managed in response to his grief.

Provide Regular Supervisor Support

The key word here is *regular*. It's not all hands on deck the first week and then back to regular programming at week two. It might take your supervisee that long or longer just to get over the shock of it all, to have the raw, unhindered feelings about their client's death begin to surface. Perhaps it's about regular, scheduled supervision for your supervisee to have the allotted time and space to process. Does it mean you need to increase your contact, be present more in the office, or offer a quick check-in as needed? Respecting your boundaries and taking the ethical parameters of supervision into account, it's still a good idea to be readily available to your supervisee after a client suicide if possible, whatever that looks like for you.

Lorel

Lorel wasn't actively seeking supervision due to being a licensed independent professional, but she did want consultation and support after her client's death by suicide. Her consultant was in agreement to weekly meetings for the first three months after her client's death, hoping to help Lorel navigate through some purposeful processing to alleviate her more disruptive somatic symptoms of tension headaches and her inability to sleep. Lorel had felt that she was slowly unraveling in the weeks before connecting with her consultant, and she was grateful for the support and structure to address her grief.

Review Case File or Notes if Desired

Reviewing a case file is all about timing and purpose. Ideally, it's on the timeline of your supervisee and when they'd like to review it. I recognize that this isn't always realistic or a good idea if they are attempting to avoid thinking about their client's death. I also recognize that the higher-ups may be breathing down your neck to do the file review to make sure no one is getting sued. Timing matters. Has your supervisee had a moment to take in this tragic news? Have they had a chance to react before we put their file and documentation under a microscope? Are they spinning out while trying to sit down and answer questions from leadership? Purpose also matters. Is the purpose of the file review to confirm or deny fault on behalf of the clinician? Is the purpose to go through their notes with a fine-tooth comb, identifying all the times they could have done something different, something more, or something better? That sounds traumatic in and of itself, right? If a case file review is optional, perhaps the clinician will state they want to review the file at a later date and choose to staff it with a supervisor or consultant at that time. For some therapists, this process feels like a piece of their healing journey, especially if some time has passed since working with the client and they want to refresh their memory on where things left off. For others, it feels like torture, no matter how much time has passed. Being aware of how a file review request lands for your supervisee is the first step to setting a thoughtful pace and clear agenda with them around the process.

Evie

Evie was six months into her online support group when she noticed an internal desire to review her case file had surfaced. She sat in it further with her trusted group members, approaching it with curiosity. Evie discovered that her purpose for reviewing the case file wasn't about identifying fault or flaws in her interaction with her teen client as their therapist; it was to review and celebrate the work they had done together before her client had died by suicide. Upon reviewing the file, Evie came back into the group the next week with fresh tears in her eyes. She expressed gratitude and awe for her client's hard work, clarity of their pain, and ongoing compassion for their suffering.

Help Therapists See Their Competencies

One of the most common responses to client suicide that we see is therapists questioning their own competency. So it becomes even more important for supervisors and mental health leaders to identify strengths and competencies for clinicians when they have grief and loss blinders on. What can you point out that is going well? Where do they continue to shine in their clinical work? What do they excel at? Adopting a strengths-based approach isn't exclusive to client work; it can work well for clinicians who need reassurance and evidence that they are still doing things of value in therapy sessions with their clients.

Alejandra

Alejandra was doing well in solo practice, but recognized she felt isolated and lonely at times. Her spiritual side was craving more connection with others, so she decided to manifest an opportunity to connect more deeply with other people in the next few months. Several weeks later, she was excited to learn she'd been accepted into the latest cohort for Level I Internal Family Systems (IFS) training after being on the waitlist for more than two years. Parts work was something she had adopted naturally into her therapy practice, and she was excited to embark on an almost week-long training experience amid other clinicians to learn more. When completing some video training content, she witnessed IFS founder Dr. Richard Schwartz echo her own beliefs about suicide and client choice. She left the training with refined skills, new friends, and a renewed sense of purpose when serving her chronically suicidal clients.

Share Similar Experiences

If, as a supervisor, you've experienced a client death by suicide, you have an unexpected gift to give your supervisee. Through your own pain and healing journey, you can help them see that a client suicide doesn't fully define them as a professional—that they aren't a lesser therapist for having a client die. For many supervisees, hearing that the trusted, competent supervisor they work closely with has also experienced a client suicide disrupts the ugly narrative they have that they themselves are incompetent. Here in front of them is a successful mental health leader, a leader who has also experienced a loss. A leader who chooses to continue to work in this field and helps the next generation of therapists called to do the same. If you don't have the lived experience of a client suicide, perhaps you can normalize it with the information found within this book. Can they hear Annabelle, Jeremy, Lorel, Evie, and Alejandra's stories and relate to them? Can they read about other experiences in other books or online? As their supervisor, you can bridge the gap between their assumptions that this doesn't happen often with the reality that it does. You are giving them a gift, which is to know they aren't alone.

Evie

Evie was feeling more ready to launch an in-person support group for therapists who'd lost a client to suicide. She knew that she wasn't the only one, that there would be more loss in her community, and she wanted to help other clinicians in ways that her online group members had helped her. Evie felt ready to share similar experiences with others by creating a safe, local space for that sharing. She knew it would involve disclosing her client loss as the facilitator of the group, and she felt grounded and prepared for that task. Evie began by telling colleagues about the group formation and started sharing her contact information with anyone who might want to learn more.

Explore Their Schedule

As mental health leaders, we can validate and normalize the pivots a clinician may require when attempting to heal from client suicide. Oftentimes, a therapist may feel that they have to push through or keep going for their clients, for their team, or for the financial stability that working provides. What if it didn't occur to them to advocate for a change? Whether it's a temporary shift or a permanent pivot, we can broach the conversation in supervision or consultation to help them further explore their options. What would it be like for them to hear that a smaller caseload is an option? What would they think about some time off to grieve and regroup? Do they need to explore their current caseload for any changes or thoughtful transfers of clients for some additional breathing room? Is paid time off available? Clinicians feel significantly altered after a client suicide; their schedule may need to reflect this in some way too.

Lorel

Through her steady work with her consultant, Lorel uncovered the missing piece for healing from her client suicide. Her client's safe space had been a remote beach in Hawaii that she had visited as a little girl before loss and trauma had ripped her family apart. One of her client's future plans had been to revisit that beach to begin writing her memoir with her feet buried in the sand. Lorel discovered that she felt called to go to that same beach as part of her grief and loss process, with plans to write and remember her client through various mindfulness activities. With some encouragement from her consultant, Lorel was able to make plans for some time off from her private practice in order to travel to that remote beach, allowing her the gift of time and space to heal herself while honoring her client's memory.

Identify Evolution in Their Client Work

Another aspect of holding the role of supervisor or consultant for a colleague who's experienced a client suicide is helping them pinpoint how they've changed. More specifically, how their clinical work has changed. It's natural for a therapist to shift their approach to suicide in response to a client death. Can we help them identify the shifts taking place? Are the shifts helping or hurting? For example, perhaps a therapist changes their approach to suicide by asking about it more frequently with the clients they engage in therapy. Maybe they adopt a streamlined assessment to help them remember all the questions to ask in a critical moment with a client experiencing suicidal thoughts. Maybe they have a visceral urge to avoid suicide, and begin to panic anytime a client appears to be declining. Or perhaps they want to avoid populations that pose greater risks for suicide. Slowing a clinician down to reflect on the subtle and not-so-subtle behavioral changes and thought patterns they are embracing as the result of a client suicide is a powerful piece of their healing work.

Jeremy

Jeremy's supervisor continued to be a grounding presence in his healing from his client's suicide. Several months into his work, his supervisor asked about how Jeremy felt he'd changed as a clinician. Jeremy was thankful to recognize he had an answer, one that surprised him when sharing it aloud. Although Jeremy had been hypervigilant and irritable for the first few months after his client's death, Jeremy had moved from holding his breath after asking the question about suicide at an intake to exhaling and being more present when waiting for a client's answer. With additional training and ongoing support from his supervisor, Jeremy was feeling more compassionate and better equipped to support his clients. His supervisor echoed the positive changes he was seeing in Jeremy, naming how his ability to breathe easier had helped him show up more authentically with his clients, leading to better therapeutic outcomes than when Jeremy was showing up in anxiety and fear about suicide in sessions.

Recognize the Tragedy and the Positive Changes That Occurred Afterward

Although change may be easiest to identify within the clinician, the ripple effect their client's suicide has on other areas of their life is worth exploring as well. As a mental health leader, can we invite clinicians to honor the tragedy of their client's death alongside the meaningful evolution they discover in themselves later? It might be years before they fully see how their client suicide shapes other aspects of their life. Acknowledging something aloud gives it power, so why not invite your supervisee to name the longer-lasting impact from the positive lens of their post-traumatic growth? Perhaps they feel called to start a support group or volunteer with a suicide prevention organization. Maybe they want to share their story on stage or in a book. Maybe they hold more compassion for folks experiencing suicide within their family or community. Perhaps they want to be a suicide trainer or speaker to help colleagues in the field. Tragedy can mean something has ended, but it can create space for new beginnings too.

Alejandra

In gaining new language from her IFS training, Alejandra felt excited to lean in even further with her clients around their suicidal parts. When she was enthusiastically sharing how several months of successful IFS work applied to chronic suicidality with a colleague, they asked if she would ever consider training other clinicians who might be interested in learning her technique. Alejandra was thrilled to be asked, as it hadn't occurred to her that other clinicians might want to learn what she was doing in therapy with her clients. She started by putting a training together for a small group of therapists, which was well received. It led to an invitation to speak again to a larger audience, which catapulted her into a successful training and public speaking career where she shared her story of client suicide with messages of hope and resilience alongside strategies for serving clients in need.

With added clarity, we know how supervisors and mental health leaders can help clinicians on their path to healing. Next, let's take a look at intentional tools for clinicians to explore on their own or with chosen supports as part of their healing work after a client suicide.

Grief Tools to Support Healing From Client Suicide   14

ALTHOUGH BY NOW you've thoroughly explored the importance of supports throughout this book, this chapter is dedicated to naming tools that can support your process independently after a client's death by suicide. What are intentional tools or practices that can aid in your efforts to lean on and lean in?

1. Craft a client letter
2. Write a dedication
3. Donate to suicide prevention
4. Light a candle
5. Release a balloon or lantern
6. Honor their birth date, death date, or other meaningful date
7. Journal thoughts and feelings
8. Engage in an intentional activity

Craft a Client Letter

The power of brain-body connection through handwritten materials remains important in therapeutic work with our clients. Why wouldn't we consider it in our own recovery after a client suicide? Encouraging multiple drafts, you may start with a letter that expresses your hurt, anger, or sense of betrayal, that naturally evolves into a letter of acceptance and closure as you do your own work. Notice how reviewing each letter at a later date shows your evolution in the process. You also have the opportunity to release the letter(s) in ways that feel meaningful for you, such as burning them or burying them in the earth when the timing feels right.

Evie

Evie ended her work in her online support group with other therapists by reading her letters to her client aloud. She started with the one most full of hurt and ended with the one that represented where she was now, a powerful contrast of pain and confusion to clarity and compassionate acceptance. Reading her letters aloud to the group cemented some things for her. It signified growth and remained a gift the group continued to give her each week through listening to her share within the safe space they'd created together. She named these reflections and expressed gratitude for all the group had given her as she prepared to leave.

Write a Dedication.

Did you know you can write a dedication to your client online or in print? There are organizations that house this offering, whether they are connected to loss through funeral services or are provided as part of suicide prevention nonprofits and donations. What would it be like to honor a client in this way? To add their name to a sentence that starts "in memory of"? Do you name them? Do you use another name? What would you include in the dedication in honor of their life, their work, and their memory after death?

Lorel

Lorel felt called to donate to a local suicide prevention nonprofit that offered dedications for people lost to suicide. It felt low risk and especially important because her client had no family left. No one else was going to do this piece in honor of her client and that didn't sit well with Lorel. So she entered the mindful space of crafting a dedication her client would have liked. She found herself imagining her client sitting across from her as she worked on it, smiling and commenting on the various parts Lorel included. This was heartfelt and meaningful for Lorel, who checked in on how she was feeling after it was submitted, and once again when she saw it posted live on the nonprofit's website.

Donate to Suicide Prevention

Whether you donate on your own or assist with fundraising efforts at a live event, suicide prevention organizations are readily available to provide additional resources, training, and materials on their mission to reduce the risks of suicide. Familiarizing yourself with trusted organizations can be a piece to your grief and loss puzzle, especially if you feel compelled to get involved in some way as part of your own healing. I also encourage mental health leaders to explore how team involvement in events and donations may be appropriate, not only to connect to a community focused on suicide prevention, but to normalize the possibilities of suicide being experienced by team members and by having outside resources readily available.

Jeremy

As the seasons changed, Jeremy was asked by his supervisor if he was interested in spearheading the treatment center's involvement in their local "Out of the Darkness" walk, a chapter event hosted by the American Foundation for Suicide Prevention (AFSP). Agencies and organizations were encouraged to participate with the goal of fundraising for suicide prevention. After taking the trip with his wife for some R&R and continued education opportunities, Jeremy felt refreshed and ready to participate in something of this scale. He agreed to be the team lead, recruited colleagues to walk laps at the event, and organized their marketing materials as a treatment center for a vendor booth to connect more closely with their community.

Light a Candle

This effort may feel simple until we focus on the intention backing the behavior. To light a candle with intention feels spiritual and grounded. It supports the importance of ritual and can become a container for some of our grief. It also makes me think of candle practices like leaving a lit candle in the window for someone to find their way home. Or a religious practice of lighting a candle in memory of someone we've lost. Or a spiritual practice of connecting with something or someone beyond our plane of existence that feels larger than ourselves. It can also, more simply, support mindfulness when staring at the gentle flame. However you conceptualize it, lighting a candle can hold meaning for honoring your client lost to suicide. Experiment with scented candles. Identify thoughts associated with lighting the candle versus blowing it out. Notice how you feel before, during, and after the candle is lit. This ritual can take on unique meaning in grief work, depending on the individual and the purpose of the flame.

Alejandra

There was no question that Alejandra would be lighting a candle when processing her client's death by suicide. As a spiritual person, Alejandra already honored her loved ones at an altar each year for All Soul's Day. She felt comfortable asking her ancestors to embrace her client's place in this day of remembering, and selected a candle for her client for the upcoming Day of the Dead.

Release a Balloon or Lantern

Another common practice within grief and loss work is to release a message or well-wish with an object in flight. Oftentimes with a balloon or lantern, folks find comfort in seeing the message gently floating higher and higher into the air, symbolizing a closer connection with the person they've lost. Other folks find comfort in believing their message has been delivered to a loved one who is now in heaven. Although that is not the primary belief or purpose of floating objects, many people find comfort in this ritual after a suicide.

Jeremy

On the day of the local suicide prevention walk, Jeremy and others were invited to gather and release a balloon for each person they'd lost to suicide. Jeremy was struck by how simple and powerful this exercise was, especially when watching thousands of balloons go up into the air at once. He experienced sadness followed by a lightness when watching the batch of colorful balloons rising gently above the event space. He noticed he was speaking his message of comfort to his client in his mind as he watched his balloon, reinforcing Jeremy's intentions of processing and releasing some of his emotions about his client's death.

Honor Their Birth Date, Death Date, or Other Meaningful Date

It would be hard to forget a date that's been cemented in your mind in some way. Like 9/11 or any other significant day of trauma or tragedy, your client's death date may also feel like it's taken up permanent residence in your mind. What if it's a day that isn't so emotionally charged? What if it's your client's birthday, or another day you associate with their life or your work together? Honoring this date means acknowledging it, preparing for it, and making it intentional. For clients in therapy, I encourage them to think of a trauma anniversary as an opportunity to listen closely to what they need. The same applies here with healing from your client's suicide. Do you need to take the day off? Do you want the structure and activities to look different from your typical day? Is it about pausing in the middle of what you are doing to acknowledge the significance of the day? Moving forward with gentleness? Being alone with your thoughts? You get to decide; otherwise your body and the memories it stores tend to decide for you.

Evie

Evie knew her client's death date was forever stamped onto her brain. She experienced anxious anticipation when she thought of the rapidly approaching one-year mark, not being 100% certain of how she'd feel. When listening to other therapists in her support group share what it was like at the one-year anniversary of their clients' deaths, she realized she wanted it to be a positive day of remembrance of her client if at all possible. She recalled how, as a dedicated athlete, their favorite cheat day food was a double cheeseburger, fries, and a chocolate shake from a local restaurant. It was something her client looked forward to and relished every time they got to indulge, bringing it up in therapy on multiple occasions. Evie decided she would engage in the mindful eating of this meal on her client's death anniversary, slowing down to savor the food while thinking of them fondly.

Journal Thoughts and Feelings

Although journaling may feel cliché because of its frequency within the therapy space, it shows up often because of its potential for deeper reflection and healing. A healthy outlet for strong emotions and heavy thoughts, capturing a person's evolution through stress, pain, and grief can be instrumental to post-traumatic growth. Journaling can be a strategy to capture and contain thoughts and feelings outside of us. It can contribute to ongoing processing and new awareness when rereading what we wrote at another time. Even if we never read it again, pouring our heart and soul onto a page can serve as a cathartic release when we would otherwise feel that we were drowning in our emotions. Don't discount the power of writing things out by hand.

Alejandra

Even though Alejandra wasn't feeling deeply distressed about her client's choice to die, she did feel motivated to journal about the experience to explore the parts of herself that were most present. Alejandra wanted to check in to ensure her manager parts (as defined in her IFS training) weren't driving her behaviors or contributing to her lack of emotional distress. She decided to journal as a way to access Self, the deepest, most rooted, and authentic version of her being. By doing so, she felt more reassured that she had healed the parts of herself that originally felt sadness or anxiety when learning of her client's suicide. Through journaling, Alejandra felt more confident that she had integrated the loss of her client into her present functioning without maladaptive behaviors getting in the way.

Engage in an Intentional Activity

The key here is to do *the thing* with intention. Whether it's walking, moving your body, trying something new, eating, or writing, if done with intention, it increases the activity's healing potential. What thing feels connected to your client? Is it visiting a place they loved? Eating a food they liked? Watching a movie they would have wanted to see? Is it trying something they had wanted to try, like axe throwing or pottery? There are so many possibilities that can come from brainstorming what feels in alignment with your client and with yourself. Pick something that feels like a homage to them while being meaningful to you.

Lorel

After several months of planning, Lorel was ready to embark on her trip to the secluded beach in Hawaii her client had talked about frequently in therapy. She had packed materials for deeper processing, including a journal, her sensory kit, walking shoes, and a meditation playlist. Lorel was prepared to sit on the sand and breathe deeply, letting her mind wander to her client and the beautiful space her client had found so safe. She wasn't sure what might surface, but Lorel felt prepared and open to take it in, knowing it would have meaning in her larger healing journey.

What grief tools would you add? By no means is this an exhaustive list, nor should they be added in a particular formula to feel like yourself again. Like any other grief event, the timeline for healing from your client's suicide is unique to you and your needs. In my own healing journey as a therapist survivor, I had the strong feeling I was going to write about my client Rena's suicide sometime in the future, so I journaled to capture the details hours and days into her death, while things were still painfully fresh. Journaling served as a review of Rena's life and the steps we took together to attempt to keep her safe. It also served as a vessel to hold my grief as I attempted to function on the outside. I share my journaled account of events leading up to Rena's death by suicide in Appendix C to illustrate another example of the complexity and impact a client's suicidal thoughts and resulting suicide can have on us as therapist professionals.

Experiencing Post-Traumatic Growth **15**

M Y SUICIDAL CLIENTS will never be forgotten; this book serves that purpose, among many other heartfelt purposes and goals. Although I wasn't successful at helping Rena find reasons to stay alive, so many of us as therapists do our damnedest to try. Rena is the exception, not the rule. So what about Tillie and Marlena? What about Evie, Alejandra, Jeremy, Lorel, and Annabelle? Where are they now? Their stories help us hold onto hope as we navigate the darkness a client death by suicide brings. Let's end things on messages of hope, compassion, and inspiration, continuing to do our best for ourselves, our communities, and the clients we serve.

Tillie
After repairing our therapeutic relationship following Tillie's hospitalization, I passed several more of her interpersonal tests in such a way that Tillie felt safe being fully real with me. She was able to name the dark moments as they happened. We were able to successfully create a safety plan around her urges to self-harm. She was willing and ready to address the origins of her self-hatred in our ongoing work together. After a time, Tillie was ready to speak her truth to her parents in family therapy, another important aspect of her healing journey. After about a year and a half of work, Tillie felt strong enough to utilize her supports of ongoing family therapy and her school counselor, so we said our heartfelt goodbyes in wrapping up our work together. Several years after that, I received a piece of mail from Tillie's mom at my office, announcing her graduation from high school. Enclosed was Tillie's senior photo, capturing her most

authentic personality and a giant smile. It was an unexpected gift to know she was doing well.

Marlena

Marlena struggled to face some hard truths in her relationships to break out of maladaptive patterns. On one hand, her relationship with her daughter had fractured, sending her spiraling into more intense suicidal thoughts at the idea of her daughter leaving her. On the other hand, she was pursuing a formerly abusive partner to have a relational tie during one of the darkest moments of her life. Marlena self-sabotaged her way out of therapy, canceling and no-showing several appointments, which voided her attendance contract and led to a discharge from services. She requested to reengage in therapy almost a year later when her daughter had relocated and she'd ended the unhealthy romantic relationship after about eight months. I provided a referral to a colleague who specialized in survivors of abuse as the better fit for Marlena's goals at that time. Marlena felt she was ready to do the harder work, exploring her self-worth and its connection to hurtful relationship patterns, self-sabotage behaviors, and chronic suicidal thoughts.

Evie

After a couple of months of marketing, Evie had a small group of therapists ready to start her in-person support group for healing from client suicide. Evie found herself flourishing in this new leadership role, as it blended her love of structure and systems from group practice ownership with the more intimate connection forged from the group's purpose and function. Clinicians who participated then shared her group with others in need of support, and she found herself facilitating several groups a month within her therapeutic community. Recently, Evie was approached by a national suicide prevention organization to explore streamlining her support group content to build a train-the-trainer program with the mission of having more in-person support groups offered regularly in multiple states. Her client's face flashed across her vision, grinning and raising their chocolate shake in a toast of approval in her mind's eye as Evie said yes to drafting up a contract for this new endeavor.

Alejandra

Seeing her training content grow in demand, Alejandra decided to make an online version of her training to reach more therapists interested in using IFS with client suicidal thoughts. She'd gathered a mailing list of almost two hundred clinicians who were waiting for the training to launch, and had received an offer to be the keynote at the next local conference in her area. When preparing to film online content or when rehearsing her keynote, Alejandra continued to light a candle for her client in the background, which burned brightly until she thoughtfully extinguished it. Each time she blew it out, she would convey a message of compassion and gratitude to her client, their work together, and her client's influence on Alejandra's professional journey of helping other therapists engage in the challenging topic of suicide.

Jeremy

Jeremy continued to participate in local suicide prevention events annually as a way of honoring his client and connecting with his community on suicide. He was encouraged by his supervisor to pursue training to become an Approved Clinical Supervisor (ACS), knowing Jeremy could help other therapists navigate client suicide within their career. Jeremy remained sober, and cravings to use again had disappeared in the months after his client's death. Jeremy recognized that he no longer had the urge to use or be numb when thinking of his client's death. Instead, he was excited to be present for this next chapter of his personal and professional journey. Jeremy was close to finishing his training hours for supervision and has been offered a position as a clinical supervisor at his current employment. He was prepared to say yes to this leadership opportunity and had intentions of celebrating this accomplishment alongside another year of sobriety with his wife over dinner.

Lorel

Lorel had a transformative experience during her time in Hawaii, having connected with her client's memory more fully and having also connected more with herself. She reflected on how she'd lost a piece of herself with her client's death, and how carving out a space to find herself again had been extremely helpful and grounding. Lorel was entertaining the idea of offering retreats for clinicians overwhelmed by grief and loss, whether it was due to a client suicide or another loss in the workplace like the death of a colleague or mentor. Lorel was brainstorming this idea with her consultant to explore the aspects that felt most authentic and meaningful to her as a potential retreat facilitator. She was enjoying the process of dreaming about how to best help other professionals, dipping her toe into this latest possibility with curiosity and compassion.

Annabelle

Although Annabelle opened up to one colleague about her client suicide, she continued to struggle with crippling fear that drove her to retreat from her professional community and made her reluctant to share her experience fully with others. Annabelle's health declined to the point where she was required to take time off from work. Even though she appeared to understand the importance of grief and loss work, confidential grief and the stigma of client suicide had kept her from fully entering her healing journey. Annabelle, if you read this, know that my colleagues and I are here for you when you are ready. I know it takes time to build trust. It takes time to find the right person to help you do this work. You don't have to suffer in silence any longer; there are colleagues who can hold this compassionately for you when the timing is right. You are not alone, and you don't have to heal alone either.

My Wishes for You

There are so many intentions behind this book being written that I hope have come through clearly in each and every chapter. Messages like:

- Suicide is complex.
- Suicide doesn't discriminate.
- Lean into your client's suicide story.
- Some therapists will have a client die by suicide.
- Confidential grief is damaging.
- Don't do this on your own.
- Mental health leaders can help clinicians.
- Do your healing work.
- *Lean on, lean in.*

If you are like Annabelle, your healing journey hasn't quite started. Maybe this book has given you the inspiration you needed to entertain the idea of opening up, owning your experience, and asking for help. If that feels true, then one of the missions of this book has been successful. I know it takes time to build trust. I know colleagues have been hurt by the responses or lack of responses from their community and colleagues after a client suicide. Don't give up on finding that person you can rely on to be compassionate and caring when speaking your truth.

I have a vision of building community and support for therapists who've had a client die by suicide. The 25%. The *therapist survivors*. Successfully eliminating confidential grief. Receiving help and empathy from folks like Jeremy and Alejandra, who are giving back through leadership roles after their own lived experiences of client suicide. Seeking out services with Evie and Lorel, who feel called to create safe spaces for therapists to do this powerful and oftentimes necessary work to remain in the profession. There is support. There are resources. You can do this. You can find yourself in post-traumatic growth one day, seeing the tragedy of your past evolve into something beautiful and profound in the present.

That's where I am when finishing this book; I'm evolving. Every book I write covers a harder, darker topic within the therapeutic arena. Not every day is a good one when I think of Rena and the life she's not living. Not every day do I feel like holding for the heaviness that is client suicide. But then I think of Tillie and Marlena and the many clients like them, and I want to try. Writing this book names my intention of wanting to be a safe person for colleagues navigating life and their career after a client suicide. Offering a space of abundant compassion and zero judgment. In order to be an effective resource to my colleagues, I continue to do my own work, revisiting the principles of LEAN when I backslide into old, unhelpful habits or when I lose my way. Listening to my needs in any given moment, embracing grief and loss work, asking for help from my most trusted colleagues, and naming my meaning. I will continue to speak on suicide assessment and I will continue to share my story of client suicide if it helps my colleagues. This lived experience of client loss to suicide gives my work even more meaning.

What meaning will you discover in your own healing journey? There's only one way to find out.

Lean on, lean in.

Appendix A
Suicide Prevention Tools and Trainings

Khara's Resources for Clinicians:

- Engage in our ALERT online training titled "Saving More Lives from Suicide" approved for NBCC 4.0 CEs at https://savinglivesseries.mykajabi.com/offers/Ga4H4BBR
- Contact Khara at mailto:croswaitecounselingpllc@gmail.com to schedule your custom 1.5–3 hour training (live or online) on ALERT suicide assessment and safety planning.
- Explore our suicide risk app available at https://cacs-co.com/, which includes access to a suicide assessment, suicide screener, safety planning template, and 1,020+ resources for clients served in Colorado.
- Review role-play videos and resources for suicide assessment and safety planning at https://croswaitecounselingpllc.com/suicideassessment

Additional Trainings in Suicide Assessment*:

- CAMS: https://cams-care.com/
- Columbia C-SSRS: https://cssrs.columbia.edu/
- LivingWorks ASIST Training: https://livingworks.net/training/livingworks-asist/
- QPR: https://qprinstitute.com/

---

* *This is not an exhaustive list, nor do I receive any compensation for featuring these resources.*

Recommended Readings for Clinicians:

- *Helping the Suicidal Person* (2018) by Dr. Stacey Freedenthal
- *Loving Someone with Suicidal Thoughts* (2023) by Dr. Stacey Freedenthal
- *Managing Suicidal Risk: A Collaborative Approach* (2016) by Dr. David Jobes
- *Why People Die by Suicide* (2005) by Dr. Thomas Joiner

Appendix B
Risk Factors for Suicide

Alter, Adam L. *Irresistible: The Rise of Addictive Technology and the Business of Keeping Us Hooked*. Penguin Books, 2018.

- Technology use and addiction: pp. 6–10
- Social isolation: p. 217

Erbacher, Terri A., et al. *Suicide in Schools: A Practitioner's Guide to Multi-Level Prevention, Assessment, Intervention, and Postvention*. Routledge, 2005.

- Grief and loss: p. 185
- Risk levels: p. 97
- Screenings: p. 185
- Threat assessment and reduction: pp. 47–48
- Warning signs: p. 103

Flemons, Douglas G., and Leonard M. Gralnik. *Relational Suicide Assessment: Risks, Resources, and Possibilities for Safety*. Norton, 2013.

- Access to firearms: p. 125
- Acute stressors: pp. 78–79
- Anorexia nervosa: p. 107
- Burden and isolation: p. 92
- Chronic risk: p. 122
- Disciplinary action for students: p. 80
- Disclosures of SI or death: p. 124
- Ending suffering or pain: p. 121

- Family conflict: p. 102
- Grief and loss: p. 92
- Humiliation and shame: pp. 92, 119
- Legal problems: p. 80
- Mental illness: p. 89
- Protective factors: p. 127
- Rejection: p. 76
- Risk levels: p. 119
- Safety planning: p. 129
- Sleep interruption: p. 95
- Therapeutic alliance: pp. 62, 119

Freedenthal, Stacey. *Helping the Suicidal Person: Tips and Techniques for Professionals.* Routledge, 2018.

- Access to firearms: pp. 72, 126
- Burden and isolation: pp. 70, 163
- Chronic risk: pp. 100, 143
- Collaborative interview: p. 67
- Consultation with colleagues: p. 134
- Demographics and suicide: p. 86
- Documentation needs: pp. 102–103
- Intensity of suicidal ideation: pp. 59, 215
- Internet searches of suicide: p. 74
- Key protective factors: p. 84
- Mini-screening tools: p. 152
- No-suicide contracts: p. 115
- Structure of safety planning: pp. 118–121, 146

Joiner, Thomas E. *Why People Die by Suicide.* Harvard University Press, 2005.

- Abuse and risk: pp. 65, 189–190
- Age: p. 162
- Anorexia nervosa: p. 196
- Burden and isolation: pp. 96, 106–107, 109
- Chronic risk: p. 61
- Depression: pp. 58, 164
- Ethnicity and culture: p.160,
- Family history: pp. 174, 176

Shea, Shawn C. *The Practical Art of Suicide Assessment: A Guide for Mental Health Professionals and Substance Abuse Counselors.* Mental Health Presses, 2011.

Twenge, Jean M. *iGen: Why Today's Super-Connected Kids Are Growing up Less Rebellious, More Tolerant, Less Happy—and Completely Unprepared for Adulthood—and What This Means for the Rest of Us.* Atria Books, 2017.

Appendix C
Getting Real About Rena

I'm not okay but I will be.

July 18, 2017

As we sit down in my office for the first time, I notice her gold-colored eyes. She's decked out in green, from the hat on her head to the phone case she holds in one hand. In her 20s, she presents her trauma story from a deadpan place. Although open to talking, she's hard to read in having limited facial expressions. As a therapist this intrigues me. I like to think I'm good at reading people. It's part of my job.

What do I note in her intake? Suicidal thoughts on and off since she was a teenager. Significant attachment traumas with family members due to physical and sexual assault in her critical years. Gaslighting. Estrangement. Threatening behaviors by former family members. She proudly shares her commitment to therapy, having worked with her last therapist for several years before referring her to EMDR trauma work here in my office.

Let's call her Rena.* Rena begins treatment goals of healing her traumas. She schedules every week and is transparent about struggling most springs with trauma anniversaries and death anniversaries that impact her mood. We discover together that her suicidal thoughts get louder during this time of year. She's open and honest, and we scale her risks to monitor her transitions between seasons.

---

* Name and identifying information have been changed to protect confidentiality.

May 29, 2018

Rena is consistent with therapy and makes progress in finalizing her goal of complete estrangement from her family for her own health and wellness. She processes the grief and loss and writes heartfelt letters. Together, we discover her love of being on the water and photography. These things bring her solace in her grief.

Of course there are some bumps along the way. Her suicidal thoughts fluctuate based on triggers of other people's actions. Triggers like being discounted, dismissed, threatened, or manipulated. Triggers like being outreached by an estranged sibling through social media and her life being threatened. Being accused of being a liar about her abuse history. Triggers like being robbed outside her job one night. Rena discovers that these interactions make her feel like it was her fault. Her brain tries to tell her that it's her fault she was abused. Her fault that she's been hurt. Her fault that she has been rejected by her family. We get to work on challenging these painful, visceral, self-hatred beliefs. She processes her emotions and learns to respond differently to her triggers, finding safety in her safe place imagery, her spouse, and positive feedback from her bosses at work.

April 11, 2019

Rena's emotional pain about wanting to get pregnant is exacerbating her symptoms. She is forthcoming about trauma anniversaries being triggering, in addition to her aunt's death anniversary every year. Rena identifies her aunt as someone she was close to until she died when Rena was a preteen. For Rena, this is when the family system rapidly declined. The combination of her aunt's death and Rena's birthday dial up her suicidal thoughts annually.

May 28, 2019

Rena has struggled with her suicidal thoughts not receding since April. Like a wave, she can usually feel them recede, giving her room to breathe. Rena reports she wants to give up. After several days of high numbers and increased intention to die, Rena is taken to the emergency room with the help of her concerned spouse. She recognizes her numbers have gone outside of the comfort zone we've identified, for both her and myself as her therapist.

May 29, 2019

I'm sitting in a suicide prevention conference in a beautiful mountain town when I'm struck by the realization that Rena may be my client to die by suicide. Her risks are so high, and she has some impulsivity that makes me nervous. Her previous attempts have been described to me as her having the thought of taking all her medications at once, then doing so, all within a matter of seconds. For me, this leads to some strong feelings of dread, shame, and anger. It's a very real possibility she could die.

On break at the conference, I've just spoken with the ER lead doctor to share my concerns and Rena's suicide history for their consideration. As I wait to hear if the medical team decides to admit her, I learn about countertransference hate. Like a punch to the gut, I realize I'm experiencing countertransference hate with Rena. Made up of aversion and malice, my aversion to her risks for suicide contributes to the intense urge to discharge her. To get her off my caseload. To find myself free of the burden of her life-and-death story. This makes me feel like a shitty therapist, and I want to do something about it. So I volunteer to role-play a suicidal client for Dr. David Jobes at this conference. Well respected in the suicide prevention community, he wants to demonstrate compassionate suicide assessment. I embody Rena for the role-play and uncover softer emotions for her as I put myself in her shoes. This interaction in front of a hundred of my colleagues has given me the gift of renewed compassion toward my client.

May 30, 2019

The conference is going well. I'm sitting outside next to a gorgeous river with my colleague. We are talking about our business hopes and dreams. As someone else trained in suicide prevention, she helps me process the possible loss of Rena to suicide. To utter my fears and concerns aloud is freeing. She too helps me rediscover my compassion. It helps to hear from the medical team that Rena is to be fully admitted to inpatient care due to her suicidal thoughts. My shoulders relax knowing she is safe and under professional supervision.

June 18, 2019

Rena is discharged from individual therapy with me in having a medical plan to be in the hospital for 30 days. The feeling of relief continues in knowing she's safe and having her medications adjusted as part of that medical care.

July 5, 2019

Rena is home from the hospital and is asking to come back to therapy. She reports her numbers reflect a better headspace, and she's excited to share that she's been accepted into a school program. Her renewed interest in photography is also promising. She's talking about her future with hope again.

July 26, 2019

Rena asks for a phone session. She processes her hurt in having hospital staff accuse her of factitious disorder when seeking medical care for symptoms of unknown origin. Although Rena's health is declining, she discloses that previous medical hospitalizations were actually suicide attempts that failed. She admits she recently named the suicide attempts to her spouse and wants to tell me as well.

March 13, 2020

A state of stress for my clients and myself. COVID-19 has hit our state, and there is a national state of emergency declared. My thoughts go to Rena. How will this affect her desires to live or die?

April 13, 2020

Rena is completing school virtually and is working toward her goals just fine! No typical triggers to trauma anniversaries this April in having the whole country feel different this year. I am pleasantly surprised, and we focus on her strengths and areas of growth.

May 28, 2020

Rena receives the long-anticipated surgery that will improve her chances of getting pregnant. It has become clearer in sessions as of late that this has been her beacon of hope, reinforcing Rena's beliefs that the surgery will lead to having a better life both physically and mentally.

July 9, 2020

Weekly complications begin with Rena's health. She is texting me updates from her hospital rooms. Rena reports frequent ER and doctor visits for stomach pain, nausea, vomiting, and low potassium levels that make her lose consciousness.

December 18, 2020

As Rena's physical health and mental health needs fluctuate, her spouse also begins to struggle. I support Rena through a crisis call regarding her spouse's escalated suicidal thoughts and intent. Rena expresses hurt and anger that he would throw this at her the day before she goes into another surgery to address her lingering medical complications.

December 20, 2020

Rena expresses relief that the surgery went well and her spouse also seems to have stabilized.

December 24, 2020

I'm with my family on Christmas Eve. Rena texts me about ongoing fights with her spouse and triggers for her own suicidal thoughts to become louder than usual. I acknowledge her pain and her numbers while also feeling protective of my time away from work. I need the break. I need the break from all my clients, including her. I gently remind her to use crisis services in my absence over the holidays, to which she agrees.

December 31, 2020

I'm again with my family for New Year's festivities. Rena texts about ongoing fights with her spouse and triggers for her own suicidal thoughts. I can tell by her tone that she is tired of fighting with her spouse. His actions appear to be wearing down her resolve to live. This worries me, but I want to hold my boundaries. I acknowledge her pain and gently remind her to use crisis services in my absence until Monday.

February 2, 2021

Rena openly acknowledges in this session that she's feeling worn down and tired of fighting. Tired of fighting with her spouse. Tired of fighting with her body and its inability to get pregnant. Tired of fighting the suicidal thoughts. She's had thoughts of giving up again. According to Rena, her spouse continues to threaten suicide daily and refuses to hear her reasons as to why he should live. Rena shares that he expects her to find reasons for him to live. She admits she sometimes just wishes he would get it over with and stop threatening her with divorce and suicide. I can only imagine what this is doing to both of them. I encourage Rena to write down some of her thoughts as a healthy means of expression and to prevent the pain from festering in her body and mind.

February 4, 2021
Rena shares the letter she's written to her spouse in our second session this week. There are clear themes of love between them. She wants him to recognize that she didn't give up fighting when the suicidal thoughts got louder for herself. She doesn't want him to give up either. She tries to communicate that the decision to live or die is up to him and she won't be responsible for it.

February 10, 2021
I receive a text from Rena that she is in the hospital for an emergency surgery. I respond that I'm thinking about her and will wait to reschedule our appointment this week.

February 11, 2021
I receive a text from Rena that her spouse has died. Suddenly. Out of the blue. I call her immediately to offer her support. She doesn't want to live. She didn't get to say goodbye. A switch has been flipped in her brain, and she names that a part of her has died with him.

February 12, 2021
I begin the process of ongoing check-ins. Rena's intention to die has escalated. I find myself reminding both her and myself of her pain and that this response is understandable on a very human level. On the inside, I'm fighting for neutrality in recognizing my own burnout of being in this place of suicide risk again with her.

February 17, 2021
In the process of finalizing the funeral for her spouse, Rena is thinking of her own death plans. It feels as if she's fixated on dying. Making the plans is what's keeping her going. Rena is sharing daily determination to die in her texts to my work cell. I struggle to honor her pain and have to set a boundary on escalating texts when I'm unable to respond fast enough. Every text from her adds to the heaviness in my heart and mind, wondering what she will say or do next.

February 18, 2021

My numbness as self-protection is failing. Rena's death by suicide feels like a real possibility. Again. I hate this feeling. I'm at my desk crying because she might die. Is this anticipatory grief? Am I doing enough for her? I've composed emails to several colleagues, asking them for guidance and consultation. Rena has texted me that she's sending her five wishes to my office. I don't quite know what this means, but it scares me. What if it's her suicide note? Will she even live past February? My spouse attempts to comfort me as he catches me crying and worrying that night.

February 19, 2021

My wonderful colleague shares times to connect by phone. I'm crying as I tell her what Rena is planning. The uncertainty and unknown are killing my spirit. The thought of her dying alone brings me to tears. My colleague remembers this client from the conference role-play and discussion in 2019 when I was processing her possible suicide then! I feel so seen and so, so tired. I'd rather feel numb. How can I blame Rena for suicide being possible when her quality of life has gotten so bad? Her body is failing her. She's alone. Her spouse is gone. She can't have a baby. Her protective factors fluctuate minute to minute. As a human being wanting to avoid pain, Rena's current state of mind makes sense to me. But I can't tell her that, or she'll think I'm supporting her wish to die.

February 25, 2021

Rena texts that she is at the hospital for what feels like the 12th time in 2021. All medical. Low potassium, losses of consciousness per her report.

February 26, 2021

I'm engaging in a professional consultation with one of the most respected suicide prevention professionals in the nation. I own it that I'm tired. I share with some surprise and relief that I don't feel responsible for Rena's life. I want to know why this is happening this way. My consultant wants to explore with me if this interaction with Rena feels like emotional blackmail. No. Rena doesn't feel manipulative to me. She says things so matter-of-factly, it's who she is. And Rena's acknowledged that she is keeping details from me to prevent me from putting her in a hospital. I don't like the uncertainty. Countertransference hate is possibly showing up again.

From this consultation, I uncover questions I wish I could ask my client:

- *Why are you including me in every step?*
- *Are you seeking my permission to die?*
- *Why are you sending me these texts that are so painful to read?*

I don't ask Rena any of them. Later in the day Rena texts that she has been discharged from the hospital. She reports staying with a friend, numbers dropping to 50%. I take a fuller breath seeing this message from her. She has no reason to lie. Lowered numbers bring me comfort as we enter the weekend.

March 4, 2021
Rena and I are in a session exploring her protective factors. She states she had promised her deceased spouse that she would finish school, so she won't die—yet. She identifies her passive death wish for an upcoming surgery where she wants to not wake up or will make plans to sabotage the ability to wake up with an active DNR in place.

March 5, 2021
Rena texts that she has graduated from her school program. It's bittersweet! I'm feeling proud of her follow-through from 2019 to now and also feel rightly nervous since this was the one thing keeping her alive. She confirms she's celebrating with a friend, which brings my shoulders down from around my ears. My head tries to reassure me that Rena won't die today.

March 8, 2021
Rena texts to share "bad news" of her next surgery not being scheduled until September. The medical team wants her poor body to recover from everything it's already been through. A time to heal. Rena discloses she's not sure she will make it until then. Her suicidal thoughts are loud.

March 9, 2021
I've been chewing on Rena's plans to use her surgery as a means of not waking up. It's not sitting well, so I decide to address it with her in our session today. I ask Rena if she realizes what dying in surgery would mean

for the other people who are there to help her. She understands that her plan would traumatize nurses and staff she respects. She wants to be a nurse. Rena rolls along with this new insight, identifying a secondary plan of how to die.

March 13, 2021

It's the weekend again. Rena has texted that she's having medical issues and is ambivalent about being seen for them because of her desire to die. Several hours later she texts that she's going to the ER per her surgeon's suggestion. In this second text, she states her desire to keep trying to find reasons to live within our work together. There's a rush of hope in me, and I respond with words of encouragement.

March 15, 2021

Rena texts that she's had a horrible meeting with her primary care doctor. She's texting that her death date is set and that she isn't going to tell me when it is. All she will say in her message is that she "probably won't live past March." I text her reassurances and apologies that she had a negative encounter with her doctor. I work hard to confirm our session time to talk about what's coming up.

March 18, 2021

We're in another phone session thanks to living in the COVID era. Rena can't risk seeing me in person at my office with her fragile medical state. She reports there are plans to return to work March 21. I allow my confusion to be known in tracking her timeline aloud. Why would she set herself up to go back to work so soon? Rena admits that she's not sure she'll make it back to work but she's going through the motions. The month anniversary of her spouse's death is fast approaching, and we both know it will be hard for her.

I engage her in a deeper conversation about her expectations of her death and her beliefs about life after death. Rena recognizes a pain response for others when she dies and quickly names how others' pain is not more important than her death wish in wanting her own pain to stop. Rena wants to be with her spouse. She reports not leaving Denver but would ghost everyone and turn off her phone on the day of her choosing when ready to die. I acknowledge what she's sharing and how I would respond. She knows I'd do a welfare check if she stopped responding to outreach from me.

What does she expect from me in this moment as her therapist? Do I say goodbye now? Pretend everything is fine and schedule our next session? I feel helpless with the tears pressing at the back of my eyes. I ask her these questions aloud. My body feels heavy as I hold my head in my hands and listen to her stubbornness. The sheer determination coming through the phone. I also feel the need to tell her of my absence this weekend. Such shitty timing for a COVID vaccine recovery plan and I don't want her thinking I don't care if I have an awful reaction and cannot respond right away. I want to be as honest with her as she is with me in this moment. This disclosure of my limited availability is not permission to do something. It's not permission to die. This is beyond hard. Rena volunteers to email or text her suicide numbers daily to show she's still alive. Not expecting a response from me. I feel a sense of gratitude at her offer.

March 21, 2021

I've finally moved from a useless state with my vaccine recovery to feeling more like myself again. Rena has texted me apologizing for missing her outreach on Saturday, reporting she accidentally slept all day. I thank her for following up and comment on how her body might have needed the rest.

March 23, 2021

I've woken up this morning realizing I haven't heard from her. Not last night like usual. I text her at 7:38 a.m. asking to check in. She's usually awake when I do session text reminders this early in the morning, but there's nothing. No response.

I recognize that she hasn't yet responded and call her at 12:47 p.m. It goes straight to voicemail. My stomach drops to my feet. This is what she said would happen on her "ghosting day" to die by suicide. I leave a calm voicemail stating a welfare check would happen if she doesn't get back to me by a certain time. She doesn't call me back.

I call the nonemergency line and state I'm a therapist. I ask for a welfare check on my client whom I believe to be suicidal. They agree to send someone out.

It's the end of my workday, and I have no missed calls. How long does it take to do a welfare check? My colleague says 40–90 minutes usually. *WTF.*

What's taking so long? I call the line a second time only to be told that no one answered the door and the responding officers found nothing suspicious, so they left.

I'm in tears once I get off the phone. I know she's dead now. My gut is telling me it's just about someone finding her body. My spouse is trying to comfort me as I hysterically shout, "I'll be damned if I let her rot alone in there!" Tears are flowing freely. The only thing that calms me is the decision to try to hunt down her neighbor's contact information the next day. Maybe she can get into the apartment? If Rena needed help, we've all failed her. It helps to have a plan, even though I know in my heart it's too late.

March 24, 2021

I awake with a plan to call and text Rena again, in complete denial that she's already dead. *She just overslept. She forgot to charge her phone. Her phone is broken, and she's getting a new one.* There has to be a rational explanation. When I call, her phone is still off. I'm sitting here thinking very hard. If she misses her scheduled appointment tomorrow, will I have more justification to cold call a neighbor? The one who helped her with her spouse's funeral service. Or do I call now? I'm paralyzed by my feelings, delaying action that would confirm what I already know to be true.

It's 3:22 p.m. when I get the voicemail from her neighbor and friend saying that Rena has died by suicide. I call her back immediately. I'm available to talk and I want to talk to her because it doesn't feel real. I hold space for this poor woman who has had to call a dozen people to tell them she has died. I give her time to process, and she's sharing all the tragic details. I can see Rena in death so clearly in my head. It's heartbreaking, but providing a space for Rena's friend to process what has happened is the least I can do for her.

I've hung up the phone after this call and immediately attempt to call my colleague who knows what's been going on with Rena; we've staffed her case multiple times now. She doesn't answer. I call my other close colleague who I know has had a client die by suicide. He texts me that he isn't yet available, being in a client session. So I call Jamie, who's been there for difficult client cases throughout my career. She's known me the longest as a mental health professional, and I need her calm strength now. As soon as I hear her voice, I ask her if she has time to talk to me. She can tell something is wrong, and I can barely get the words out as I start to sob. I keep saying I'm sorry. She says I don't have to apologize for being devastated. I'm sorry, I say. I'm so sorry. Then I realize I'm apologizing to Rena. Over and over and over.

After a little while on the phone, Jamie has to get back to her clients, and my other colleague has called me back. He lets me cry as I tell him I've joined the ranks of therapists who have lost a client to suicide. I'm part of the statistic now. He assures me I've done nothing wrong. I tell him I'm grateful to talk about it because I don't want my spouse to get the brunt of my grief after work today. He's already helped me so much in the last month of navigating Rena's suicidal thoughts.

When my spouse finishes up his workday, he finds me sitting at the kitchen table. I can't hold back the next wave of grief. Grief that somehow sees his appearance downstairs as permission to be let loose. It's safe. I crumple over and cry. He's next to me, holding on as I let it gush out of me. As this next wave of emotion recedes, I tell him I'm going to ground myself with paperwork and set things in order in the home office. It will be calming and steadying for me.

When my first colleague calls me back that night, she knows what has happened. She said she saw my missed call and just knew. She gives me the space to process this tragedy a third time before bed. I'm heart-tired, wide awake, and grateful.

March 25, 2021

I wake up knowing Rena is dead. My face feels like stone, and my movements are slow. My spouse asks if I'm okay. "No, my client is still dead," I reply coldly. He doesn't deserve to be the target of my emotions. I give myself a pep talk. I'm going to get through this day and be grateful to have tomorrow off, I tell myself. I'm grieving.

The moments between appointments are the worst. Grief pushes at the backs of my eyes, and I swallow it down around the constant lump in my throat. I discover music is my friend in these moments. It drowns out the quiet and silences the sadness. I find myself moving my body to the music and am feeling better for it.

March 26, 2021

I've cried in the shower this morning so my spouse won't see. This grief is a process, and I have hours of normalcy in between. I've felt compelled to write her story as part of my grief journey so here we are, back at the kitchen table, writing things out.

The mantra in my head is, *I'm not okay but I will be.*
I'm not okay but I will be.
I'm not okay but I will be.
It was her mantra for a moment. Now it's mine.

References

American Association of Suicidology. (2023). https://suicidology.org/facts-and-statistics/

American Institute of Stress. (2022, February 11). *Holmes-Rahe stress inventory.* https://www.stress.org/holmes-rahe-stress-inventory

Blanchard, M., & Farber, B. A. (2020). "It is never okay to talk about suicide": Patients' reasons for concealing suicidal ideation in psychotherapy. *Psychotherapy Research, 30*(1), 124–136, https://doi.org/10.1080/10503307.2018.1543977

Castro Croy, A. (2022). Not my chicken. TEDx Adams County. https://www.ted.com/talks/alex_castro_croy_not_my_chicken

Centers for Disease Control and Prevention. (2023, August 10). *Suicide data and statistics.* https://www.cdc.gov/suicide/suicide-data-statistics.html

Cerel, J., Brown, M. M., Maple, M., Singleton, M., van de Venne, J., Moore, M., & Flaherty, C. (2018). How many people are exposed to suicide? Not six. *Suicide and Life-Threatening Behavior, 49*(2), 529–534. https://doi.org/10.1111/sltb.12450

Compton, L., & Patterson, T. (2023, September 18). Essential skill development for meaningful social connection. *Counseling Today.* https://ct.counseling.org/2023/09/essential-skill-development-for-meaningful-social-connection/

Freedenthal, S. (2018). *Helping the suicidal person: Tips and techniques for professionals.* Routledge.

Freedenthal, S. (2023). *Loving someone with suicidal thoughts: What family, friends, and partners can say and do.* New Harbinger Publications.

Gorchynski, J., & Anderson, S. (2006). Access to firearms among Orange County youth: A school-based study. *California Journal of Emergency Medicine, 7*(3), 43–46.

Hammond, L. K. (1991). "Attitudes of selected health professionals toward suicide: Relations to specialty, professional experience, and personal history." *Dissertation Abstracts International,* 52(3-B), 1777.

Joiner, T. E. (2005). *Why People Die by Suicide.* Harvard University Press.

Kaufman, S. B. (2020, April 20). Post-traumatic growth: Finding meaning and creativity in adversity. *Scientific American* Blog Network. https://blogs.scientific american.com/beautiful-minds/post-traumatic-growth-finding-meaning-and -creativity-in-adversity/

Kessler, R. C., Chiu, W. T., Jin, R., Ruscio, A. M., Shear, K., & Walters, E. E. (2006). The epidemiology of panic attacks, panic disorder, and agoraphobia in the National Comorbidity Survey Replication. *Archives of General Psychiatry, 63*(4), 415–424. https://doi.org/10.1001/archpsyc.63.4.415

Marlatt, G. A. (1996). Harm reduction: Come as you are. *Addictive Behaviors, 21*(6), 779–788. https://www.sciencedirect.com/science/article/abs/pii/0306460396000421

McAdams, C. R. III, & Foster, V. A. (2000). Client suicide: Its frequency and impact on counselors. *Journal of Mental Health Counseling, 22*(2), 107–121.

Moyes, J. (2012). *Me before you.* Penguin Books.

Salpietro, L., Ausloos, C. D., Clark, M., Zacarias, R., & Perez, J. (2023). Confidential grief: How counselors cope with client suicide. *Journal of Counseling & Development, 101*(4), 461–474. https://doi.org/10.1002/jcad.12484

Schwartz, R. C. (2023). *No bad parts: Healing trauma and restoring wholeness with the internal family systems model.* Vermilion.

Shea, S. (2011). *The practical art of suicide assessment: A guide for mental health professionals and substance abuse counselors.* Mental Health Presses.

Sherman, L. (2019, November 6). *Means safety.* American Association of Suicidology. https://suicidology.org/means-safety/

Stanley, B., & Brown, G. (2008). Stanley-Brown safety plan. https://suicidesafety plan.com/forms/

Twenge, J. (2017). *iGen: Why today's super-connected kids are growing up less rebellious, more tolerant, less happy—and completely unprepared for adulthood—and what this means for the rest of us.* Atria Books.

U.S. Department of Health and Human Services. (2023). *Warning signs of suicide.* National Institute of Mental Health. https://www.nimh.nih.gov/health/publications/warning-signs-of-suicide

Weiner, K. (2005). *Therapeutic and legal issues for therapists who have survived a client suicide.* Routledge.

Index

About the Author

Khara Croswaite Brindle, MA, LPC, ACS, CFT-I, is passionate about turning pain points into possibilities for mental health professionals and financial therapists. She is a TEDx speaker, consultant, licensed mental health therapist, professor, and financial therapist in Colorado. Her mission is to provide quality products and services to mental health professionals that spark curiosity and possibilities in alignment with professional growth and work-life balance. Khara values giving back to the next generation of therapists through teaching, consultation, and clinical supervision. She has served her community as a dedicated suicide assessment trainer and speaker both nationally and internationally since 2017. Khara's passion for suicide prevention includes training hundreds of mental health professionals on suicide assessment and safety planning, creating the CACS Suicide Risk Tool for helping professionals, and founding Catalively (2018–2021), a nonprofit focused on reducing youth suicide in Colorado.

Milton Keynes UK
Ingram Content Group UK Ltd.
UKHW020424050624
443728UK00005B/109